RIGHTING CANADA'S WRONGS:

Japanese Canadian Internment in the Second World War

Pamela Hickman and Masako Fukawa

JAMES LORIMER & COMPANY LTD., PUBLISHERS

TORONTO

James Lorimer & Company Ltd., Publishers
acknowledges the support of the Ontario
Arts Council. We acknowledge the financial
support of the Government of Canada through
the Canada Book Fund for our publishing
activities. We acknowledge the support of the
Canada Council for the Arts, which last year
invested $20.1 million in writing and publishing
throughout Canada. We acknowledge the
Government of Ontario through the Ontario
Media Development Corporation's Ontario
Book Initiative.

Library and Archives Canada Cataloguing in
Publication

Hickman, Pamela
     Japanese Canadian internment during the
Second World War / Pamela Hickman and
Masako Fukawa.

(Righting Canada's wrongs)
Includes bibliographical references and index.
Issued also in electronic format.
ISBN 978-1-55277-853-1

     1. Japanese Canadians--Evacuation and
relocation, 1942-1945--Juvenile literature.
2. World War, 1939-1945--Japanese
Canadians--Juvenile literature. 3. World War,
1939-1945--Prisoners and prisons, Canadian--
Juvenile literature. 4. Japanese Canadians--
History--20th century--Juvenile literature. I.
Fukawa, Masako, 1940- II. Title. III. Series:
Righting Canada's wrongs

D768.155.C35H52 2011   j940.53'1771
C2011-901730-X

James Lorimer & Company Ltd., Publishers
317 Adelaide Street West, Suite 1002
Toronto, ON, Canada
M5V 1P9
www.lorimer.ca

Printed and bound in Hong Kong.

*To the nisei (second-generation Canadians) who suffered
humiliation with endurance and dignity and left a proud
legacy for future generations.*

— Masako

Acknowledgements

*In 1942, Canada sent a lot of kids to camp — internment camp.
Those under sixteen years of age numbered 7,548. There were 1,371
students who were older. All were born in Canada to parents of Japanese descent who had lived in British Columbia for several decades.
When the Canadian government invoked the War Measures Act to
uproot and dispossess Japanese Canadians living on the west coast,
their lives were changed irrevocably.*

*My thanks to the five nisei who generously shared their stories for
this book. Mary Ohara was one of the first to be removed from the
100-mile "security zone." She lived on Salt Spring Island in the Gulf
of Georgia between Vancouver Island and the BC mainland. June
Fujiyama from Cumberland on Vancouver Island soon followed. They
were incarcerated in Hastings Park before being relocated inland.
Akira Horii lived in "Japantown" in Vancouver. Mary (Haraga)
Okabe lived on a farm in the Fraser Valley. Mickey (Nakashima)
Tanaka's family also owned a farm in nearby Mission. They were
among the 21,000 of Japanese ancestry stripped of their civil rights
and forcibly removed from their homes.*

*Thanks also to my husband, Stan, who scanned the photographs and
was the troubleshooter for my computer. Most of all, I thank him for
his patience, his guidance, and his continued support.*

— Masako Fukawa

*I'd like to thank a number of sources who helped with the photo re-
search for this book. In particular, Masako and Stan Fukawa for their
personal contributions, Sara Rainford, Linda Reid of the Japanese
Canadian National Museum, the Nikkei Internment Memorial
Centre, The Langham Museum, Greenwood Museum, the National
Association of Japanese Canadians, the Vancouver Public Library,
City of Vancouver Archives, Canadian War Museum and Library
and Archives Canada. Thanks also to artist Roger Shimomura for
permission to reproduce his painting, Yellow Peril.*

— Pamela Hickman

Contents

British Columbia
Canada

Prince Rupert

Ikeda Bay

Queen Charlotte Islands

Revelstoke

Slocan

New Denver

Sandon

East Lillooet

Greenwood

Lake Louise, AB

Vancouver

Lemon Creek

Englewood

Kaslo

Haney

Nelson

Vancouver Island

Mission

Cumberland

Cranbrook

Nanaimo

Tashme

Ucluelet

Abbotsford

Steveston

New Westminster

Gulf of Georgia

Galiano Island

Surrey

Chemainus

Fraser River

United States

Salt Spring Island

Moresby Island

Victoria

Kyoto

Hiroshima

Japan

Tokyo

Yokohama

Nagasaki

Wakayama Prefecture

Mirozu

Kumamoto

Introduction

Beginning in the late 1870s, thousands of Japanese people came to Canada seeking a better future for themselves and their families. They fished, farmed, worked in lumber mills, and opened businesses. Despite widespread anti-Asian feelings in British Columbia, many of these immigrants prospered and raised new generations of Japanese Canadians. But their lives were turned upside down on December 7, 1941, when Canada declared war on Japan following the Japanese bombing of Pearl Harbor. Overnight, all those of Japanese origin and descent were labelled enemy aliens. In 1942, the Government of Canada ordered the evacuation of all Japanese-Canadian men, women, and children from the west coast. They were stripped of their homes, their businesses, and any possessions they could not carry. Men and boys over sixteen were sent to road camps. The elderly, women, and children were put in internment camps in the interior of BC. Some families chose to stay together and move to the prairies where they were used as cheap farm labour. A few left everything behind and headed to eastern Canada where they could start again.

The children who suffered the internment are seniors today. For more than forty years they lived with the shame that their country had turned on them, treated them like enemies, and taken away their rights — all because of their race. Finally, in 1988 the Canadian government apologized and admitted that its racist policies were wrong.

In this book you will meet five Japanese Canadians who lived through the internment as young people. Some still feel the sting of the racism they grew up with; others look back without bitterness. They tell their stories to help you understand how easily such a terrible decision can be made, and how it affects many generations.

Kazuyo "Mary" Ohara was born in 1929 on Galiano Island between Vancouver Island and the mainland of BC. When she was eight, she moved with her family to nearby Salt Spring Island. In 1942, they were one of six or seven Japanese-Canadian families living there. Her popularity at school vanished when she was declared an enemy alien. Mary and her family were sent to Hastings Park in Vancouver and then interned in Lemon Creek in the Kootenays. At the end of the war, Mary's family was exiled to Japan, where more tragedy awaited them.

Miyoshi "Mickey" Nakashima was born in Mission City, BC, in 1927 on her family's farm. Her father, Teizo, left his birthplace in Hiroshima, Japan, at age seventeen and sailed for the United States, only to find its borders closed to Japanese immigrants. When the ship docked in Hawaii, he got off and worked at a sugar cane plantation for about six months. He heard of opportunities in Canada and left for Vancouver; he arrived in September 1907, a few days after the anti-Asian riot. After working in logging, on the railroad, and in orchards in the Okanagan Valley, Teizo had saved enough to buy land. By the 1930s his berry farm employed several hired hands. The Nakashimas were well-established and respected in the farming community in the Fraser Valley. That all changed when they were declared enemy aliens. Mickey's family lost everything and headed east to work in terrible conditions on an Alberta farm.

Akira Horii's parents had lived in BC since their arrival in the 1920s from Mirozu, a small fishing village in the Wakayama area of Japan. His father helped to build a thriving cod fishery and establish the first multi-ethnic fishing association, the BC Cod Fishermen's Co-op. The Horii family lived in Japantown, an area around Powell Street in Vancouver. It had the largest concentration of Japanese people in Canada and was the bustling nerve centre of the Japanese-Canadian community. After his father's fishing boat was taken away and they were ordered to leave the coast, Akira and his family ended up in East Lillooet, a self-supporting internment camp in the BC interior. Strangely enough, baseball helped make their harsh new life easier to bear.

June Fujiyama (not her real name) was born in Cumberland, BC, in 1922. When she was five years old, her father was killed in a mining accident, leaving her mother to raise the family on a small pension from the mining company. In 1942, around 500 Japanese families still lived in "Japantown #1 and #5," areas numbered from the mine shafts where they worked. They formed a close community of relatives and friends. June had recently finished high school and was working in the home of a white family. She was expected to find a local Japanese boy to marry, but June never imagined that she would meet her future husband in a ghost town.

Mary Teiko Haraga was born in Abbotsford, BC, in 1928, the second oldest of ten children. Her grandfather Haraga immigrated to BC from Kumamoto, near Nagasaki in Japan, at the end of the nineteenth century. In 1912 he asked his sons, including Mary's father Minato, to join him in Vancouver. After working in sawmills for several years, Grandfather Haraga and his sons saved enough money to buy land in the Fraser Valley. They cleared the land, planted fruit, and raised chickens. Mary's mother Tsuruko arrived from Japan in 1925 to marry Minato. She was seventeen years old. The couple's parents were friends and Tsuruko had been promised as a bride to Minato from the time she was born. The Haraga family was one of five Japanese farming families in the Abbotsford area in 1941. Soon they would lose everything that they had worked so hard for.

CHAPTER 1
COMING TO CANADA

Seeking a Better Future

Japan in the early part of the twentieth century did not hold a lot of opportunity. Many young men, especially those in rural areas, had few prospects for a better future. They could stay out in the country and be tenant farmers like their fathers, barely eking out a living and struggling with poor crops, famine, and disease. They could move into the overcrowded cities, where their chances were no better. Or they could risk it all and board a ship, work their way across the ocean, and begin a new life abroad. Frustration with life in Japan caused some of the most adventurous, or desperate, teens and men to "go for it."

Rice riots
Life for the peasants did not improve. Many were starving despite their hard work, so they finally rebelled. The 1918 rice riots, shown in this twentieth-century painting, were a result of terrible living conditions.

Poverty and starvation
Sadly, soup lines, like this one, were brought about by high rents, poor crops, and a system where the poor had little chance to raise themselves up.

Paying taxes
Peasant farmers made so little money that paying taxes in cash was nearly impossible. Farmers like the ones in the painting paid a percentage of their crop as a form of tax. This left them with even less to sell or eat themselves.

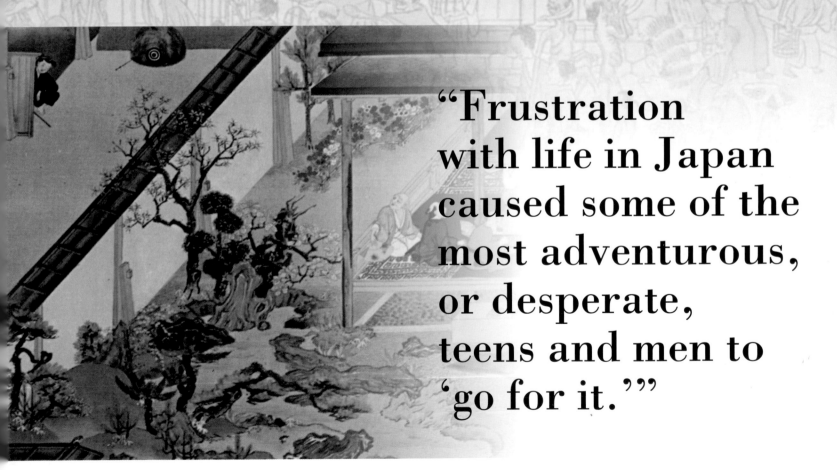

"**Frustration with life in Japan caused some of the most adventurous, or desperate, teens and men to 'go for it.'**"

The money gap
Although many Japanese people were desperately poor, some had money. This painting of Kyoto shows how the larger cities had many rich merchant homes and businesses. The gap between the rich and poor was huge and nearly impossible to cross. For many, leaving Japan seemed to be the only way to a better future.

Who Were the Immigrants?

Leaving one's home and family to set sail for an unknown land took great courage, a sense of adventure, or a need to escape the land of one's birth. Perhaps all three were at play for the Japanese immigrants who came to Canada, many of them young men in their teens. Some followed their fathers, some had dreams of money and honour, and others were just desperate to escape oppressive poverty. And some got here quite by accident.

Nowhere to go

In this woodblock print from 1833 we see a beautiful landscape but also the sadness and poverty of the peasant class. Since it was illegal to leave Japan at the time, poor people had nowhere to go and could only dream of a better life. But once the restrictions on emigration were lifted, those dreams could be pursued — even as far as Canada.

"Leaving one's home and family to set sail for an unknown land took great courage."

Ready to leave

This 1880 photo shows a crowd of Japanese emigrants waiting to board a ship bound for Canada. Among them are likely some draft dodgers. These teenage boys left home to avoid the two years of military service the Japanese government made law for all males when they turned twenty.

"Many of them were on their way to America, but some would end up in Canada."

Arrivals from Hawaii

The steamer *Kumeric*, seen here in 1907, pulled into harbour in British Columbia. On board were hundreds of Japanese immigrants who had sailed from Hawaii. Many of them were on their way to America, but some would end up in Canada.

A new adventure

It was a common sight to see the *Kumeric* pull into dock in Vancouver. Not all the immigrants on board were peasants. Some highly educated and wealthy men came to Canada, inspired by a longing for adventure. They often ended up being leaders in their new communities.

Shipwrecked

These men on the shore of Moresby Island, BC, in 1917, were the unfortunate crew of the *Kotohira Maru*, which was shipwrecked off the Queen Charlotte Islands. Adrift in a lifeboat, they were lucky to be picked up and brought ashore by another boat. Some found passage home, but it is believed that others liked what they saw and stayed.

Who Were the Immigrants?

Why Canada?

Before 1868, it was against the law for Japanese citizens to leave their country. Then, with a change in government, they were encouraged to travel overseas to earn money and learn skills that they could bring home. A nineteen-year-old boy named Manzo Nagano, who jumped ship in Westminster, BC, in 1877, is known as the first Japanese man to immigrate to Canada. He began a new life as a fisherman and later became a successful businessman. Many more Japanese immigrants followed, encouraged by the stories and successes of Nagano and other Japanese pioneers. In 1887, a regular steamship began running between Yokohama, Japan, and Vancouver, British Columbia.

Come to Canada
The sight of millions of salmon in the Fraser River was all it took to convince Gihei Kuno, pictured here, that Canada was the place where dreams came true. After he arrived in 1887, he sent word back to the people in his Japanese village that they should leave their struggles and come to Canada. Thousands came to Steveston, BC, to fish and work in the many canneries.

"Thousands came to Steveston, BC, to fish and work in the many canneries."

Canada by default

For many Japanese immigrants, like those pictured here, Hawaii was a step in their plan to go to the United States. But Californians objected to the growing number of Japanese immigrants in their cities, so the US government closed its doors to the Japanese in 1907. As a result, many came to Canada instead. About 7,600 Japanese immigrants arrived in BC in 1907.

Working in the cannery

The Celtic Cannery was one of dozens of canneries at the mouth of the Fraser River that were happy to hire newly arrived Japanese workers. The cannery also provided bunkhouses where the workers could live.

Mines need workers

Ikeda Mines Ltd., a copper mine at Ikeda Bay, was owned by a Japanese entrepreneur, Arichika Ikeda, who had left the herring business in Nanaimo, BC, to take up mining. Ikeda was lucky enough to discover the outcrop of copper on Moresby Island in the Queen Charlottes. In the early 1900s he employed up to 150 miners, many of whom were brought in from Japan. The mine closed in 1920 due to a huge drop in the price of copper.

Sawmill workers wanted

The Hastings Sawmill, pictured here in 1892, was one of the first Vancouver companies to hire Japanese workers. Business was booming and the industry needed good workers, so the sawmill hired any Japanese men who wanted a job. Many Japanese employees settled on nearby Powell Street, where cheap rooms were available. The concentration of Japanese immigrants led that area of the city to earn the nickname of Japantown.

Japanese women came too

Most of the first Japanese immigrants were single men. When they wanted to marry, many sent a photo home to family members who would use the picture to find them a wife. "Picture brides," like the two in this photo from 1915, began arriving by boat from Japan around 1908 and continued to come until 1928. In 1913, between 300 and 400 Japanese picture brides came to Canada. The women were often teachers or nurses — more educated and skilled than their husbands-to-be. Many were shocked when they arrived in the wilds of British Columbia. Sometimes, they discovered that they had been tricked into marrying someone who did not match the picture or lifestyle that had been promised to them. But they had no way of going back home. Another group of young Japanese women — often poor and illiterate — were sent to Canada by their families to earn money to send back home. They were recruited to work in brothels in Victoria, Nelson, Cranbrook, and other rail or mining towns from the 1890s onward.

"When they wanted to marry, many sent a photo home to family members who would use the picture to find them a wife."

Born in Canada

In 1885, Washiji Oya came to Canada and realized his future lay here. Within two years he had returned to Japan, married, and brought back a new bride. With them came her two sisters and a fourteen-year-old niece, all of whom married and settled in Canada to raise families. Oya's sons, pictured here with their father, were among the first nisei, or second-generation Japanese-Canadians.

Why Canada?

A Very British Society

The very name British Columbia reflected the society of early twentieth century Canada and its most western province. Canada was a proud member of the British Commonwealth, and many of its white majority of citizens had direct ties to Britain. The British Union Jack was also the Canadian flag and children sang "God Save the King" to open each school day. Increased immigration from Asia was not welcomed by the very British majority. Japanese immigrants faced legislated racism, unfair living and working conditions, and a population that wanted them gone. Even fellow members of the British Commonwealth were not welcome if they were not white (those from India, for example).

Welcome to white immigrants
In this 1903 political cartoon, the Government of Canada promotes the immigration of Europeans and British Commonwealth citizens, but only white ones. India was a member of the Commonwealth at the time, but there are no Asians pictured in the illustration.

— 1903 —

"ALL TOGETHER"

Issued by Minister of the Interior Clifford Sifton to promote immigration to Canada.

A royal celebration
In celebration of the coronation of British King George V in 1911, this Vancouver home was decorated with Union Jacks. The young girl in the centre is dressed up in a long flowing cape and crown of flowers to complete the picture of a society devoted to the royal family.

Fun at the beach
These kids are having fun at the beach in Vancouver's Stanley Park in the 1900s. The parasols, girls' fancy dresses, and boys' hats and ties reflect a very Victorian British style.

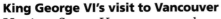

The white authority
The 1903 Vancouver Police Department reflected the authorities of the day: all white and all male.

King George VI's visit to Vancouver
Hastings Street, Vancouver, was decorated with Union Jacks to celebrate the royal visit of King George VI and Queen Elizabeth (the parents of Elizabeth II) in 1939. The visit took place shortly before the outbreak of World War II and Britain was counting on Canada's support in the event of war.

A white majority
This photo of students and teachers outside their schoolhouse in Quatsino Sound, BC, reflects the white majority of most of the province in the early 1900s.

A Very British Society   19

CHAPTER 2
JAPANESE CANADIANS IN BC, 1900–1939

Starting Out

When young Japanese men came to Canada, they were willing to take on long hours and hard work. They had left behind a life of struggle and hardship and were ready to do whatever it took to be successful in their new country. Many were already skilled fishermen back in Japan and found work in the fishing industry on Canada's west coast, either in the boats or at one of the dozens of canneries. Other natural-resource industries, such as logging and mining, were major employers of Japanese immigrants.

Skilled labour
Often Japanese men started out in the fishing industry, like these herring fishermen in Nanaimo, BC, in the early 1900s. Their talent for the job was quickly recognized and they were in great demand.

Doing the dirty work
Mining was a dirty and dangerous job. Not everyone was willing to do it. These Japanese miners at the Canadian Collieries in Cumberland, BC, (shown in 1920) were some of the many immigrants who worked in the industry.

Cannery work
This 1917 cannery receipt is a record of the fish sold to the cannery and signed for by a Japanese cannery worker.

At your service
Some Japanese men chose to work in the service sector rather than the rougher resource industries. This 1927 photo from Lake Louise shows Japanese bellboys, who were common at most of the big hotels in western Canada at the time.

"Japanese workers could be paid less than local white men."

Early days in the logging industry (opposite page)
Logging has long been a major industry in BC. Several Japanese loggers are pictured here near New Westminster, circa 1900. Compare the enormous tree trunk behind the men with the hand tools they used to fell and process it.

Remote settlements
Sawmills, like this one in Englewood on Vancouver Island, and pulp mills were large employers of Japanese workers. Since the mills were often located in back-country areas, they lost many local employees who wanted to be closer to the cities. Japanese workers, however, were not only willing to settle in remote areas, but could be paid less than local white men.

Women's Work

While Japanese men flocked to the mining, logging, and fishing industries, there were far fewer places where a Japanese girl or woman could work. If a woman lived in the back country, it was even harder to find a job than in the cities where Japanese business owners might employ her. June Fujiyama was born in Cumberland, BC, in 1922. She grew up in a tight-knit Japanese mining community and was keenly aware of how limited her future chances were. "Children grew up with a strong sense of security, but dreaming of 'what I want to do when I grow up' was futile. If lucky, a nisei girl could work as a clerk in a 'white' store if she knew the owner, but the only job open was as domestics in Caucasian homes. Girls were expected to find someone to marry, most likely a millhand, logger, fisherman, or farmer since the professions were largely closed to nisei men also."

Family business
Koji Nakasuka and his family were the first nikkei, or people of Japanese origin, to own and operate a dry-cleaning business in Vancouver, shown here in 1909. Wives and daughters often worked in family businesses.

Double duty
Many women went to work in the canneries along Canada's west coast while their husbands fished or also worked in the cannery. In this 1913 photo, you can see several Japanese women bent over the cannery assembly line with their babies wrapped up on their backs. A toddler sits in a stroller near his mother.

Sewing schools

One of the more common ways for Japanese women to earn an income was to take up sewing for pay. The women shown here are students at one of the many Japanese sewing schools that sprang up in Vancouver in the early part of the twentieth century.

Bay. 539

4243 DUNBAR ST. VANCOUVER, B. C.

MODERN DRESSMAKERS

"Bonnie Lass" Cleaners

2 for 1 Everyday

Suits, Over-Coats, Plain Dresses Our Specialty

HATS CLEANED & BLOCKED

Ladie's & Gent's Garments Cleaned Pressed & Repaired First Class Workmanship Satisfaction Guaranteed

Dressmaking & Alterations Specialty Repairing at Reasonable Prices.

MISS S. TANAKA

Owner-operator

This 1930s advertisement for Bonnie Lass Cleaners names the proprietor as Miss Tanaka (bottom right). It was not unusual for a Japanese woman to own and operate her own business at the time, especially in traditional "women's work," such as cleaning or dressmaking.

Shopkeeping

Japanese store owners hired local Japanese women to work as clerks. Here a woman tends the counter in a candy store on Powell Street in Japantown, Vancouver, circa 1937.

Success and Independence

Some Japanese immigrants and their children were able to save enough money to buy their own fishing boat or farm. Once they had this measure of independence, there was always lots of hard work to ensure success. Many first-generation immigrants, or issei, worked at more than one job in order to succeed. For instance, some farmed and fished, or farmed while working in a sawmill. After the salmon season was over, some fishermen turned to making charcoal for the canneries. Some Japanese Canadians had their own businesses, including fish-packing plants, construction companies, retail stores, and lumber and boat-building companies. Others put their energy and abilities into organizing fishing or farming co-operatives, which gave Japanese Canadians greater economic strength and protection against unfair practices.

First to farm

Jiro Inouye was a well-educated businessman. He came to Canada with his wife via the US in 1907. Giving up his business career for farming, Inouye became the first Japanese immigrant to own his own land in Haney, BC. After establishing his berry farm he encouraged others to come, buy land, and start their own farms. In 1919, Inouye formed the first Japanese farmers' co-operative in Haney, helping others to establish themselves successfully.

Burrard Fish Company
The Japanese owners of the Burrard Fish Company in Vancouver are pictured in front of their business.

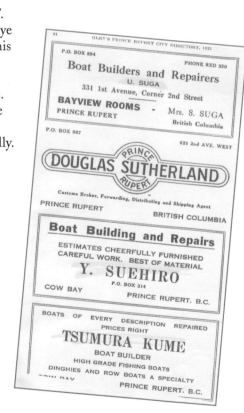

Building success
These ads in a local newspaper from Prince Rupert, BC, feature two Japanese boat-building companies. When Japanese fishermen could afford to own a boat, they would choose a Japanese boat builder to make it for them.

Royston Lumber Company
The Royston Lumber Company on Vancouver Island, shown here in 1920, was bought by Japanese Canadians in 1916. They ran it successfully as a sawmill and logging operation.

"Many issei worked at more than one job in order to succeed."

Boat-building business
Boat building was an industry that Japanese Canadians excelled at. This photo features a boat built by Hisaoka Boat Builders of Vancouver, around 1920.

Fresh produce for sale
This photo shows a produce truck from Y. Yashiki farms in 1926 on delivery in Steveston, where many Japanese immigrants settled to work in the canneries and fishing industry. Fresh fruit and vegetables were such an important part of the Japanese diet that local farmers had a large customer base in communities like Steveston.

Japantown business
Retail businesses owned by Japanese Canadians, like this gift store on Powell Street in Japantown, 1928, sprang up as individuals could afford to buy commercial properties. These businesses created more employment for Japanese people, especially women, and also provided a place where Japanese Canadians could shop for familiar articles imported from Japan.

The family farm

On a family-owned farm, children and their parents alike worked hard. This farmer, pictured in 1938, is plowing his berry field.

F. Koyama and Company, Nanaimo

Frank Koyama worked in the herring industry in Nanaimo, BC, for six years before opening F. Koyama and Company. Koyama's wholesale fish business is pictured here in 1935 alongside his private wharf residence. As his business thrived, Koyama expanded to include a general store and an ice-making plant. At one point he had sixteen fishing boats supplying him daily with salmon and cod. In turn, he supplied local markets as far away as Vancouver with fish. His company is credited with helping to build a thriving community in Nanaimo.

"(they) cleared their acreage stump by stump, stone by stone..."

Stump by stump

Mary Haraga's grandfather worked in sawmills around Vancouver and Abbotsford until he and his sons saved enough money to buy land in the Fraser Valley. Like the workers on the Fukawa farm, pictured here in the 1930s, they had to prepare the land for it to be suitable for farming. Mary's grandfather and his sons cleared their acreage stump by stump, stone by stone, a small parcel at a time. Each year they added crops of strawberries, raspberries, and rhubarb. They also raised some chickens. By the 1940s, the Haragas were one of five Japanese-Canadian farming families in the Abbotsford area.

Fear of Immigrants

Nearly 8,000 Japanese people immigrated to Canada in 1907. The phrase "Asian invasion" became widely used in the media, along with the term "yellow peril." Citizens of BC were already unhappy with the Chinese immigrant population, and saw Japanese immigration as an additional threat to their jobs and European culture. The high unemployment rate was blamed on immigrants, and fear of being overrun by Asians led to the formation in Canada of the Asiatic Exclusion League, a group that had already formed in the United States. Rumours of even more immigration from the Far East fuelled the panic that resulted in the Vancouver Riot of 1907.

Keep it white
Famous British author Rudyard Kipling is featured in the centre of this 1907 political cartoon. He agrees with the majority view at the time, that keeping BC "white" was the best policy.

HAPPY THOUGHT!
(Rudyard to the Rescue.)
"I have it! Listen, now. Cram the country full of your own kinspeople, and there simply won't be room for the Asiatics!"

NOTRE IMMIGRATION!
CB: Wilfrid, protège-moi contre ces maudites bêtes!

"The limit was reduced to 150 and changed to include all family members."

Do something!

The surge of immigration from Japan to Canada was not welcome in BC. This cartoon shows a BC politician appealing to Prime Minister Wilfred Laurier to do something about the "swarms" of Japanese immigrants. The result was the Hayashi-Lemieux, or Gentlemen's Agreement of 1908 between Canada and Japan. Japan agreed to limit emigration to Canada. Those allowed were prior residents of Canada and their families; students, merchants, tourists, and travellers in transit; farm labourers or domestic servants who worked for Japanese employers in Canada; or labourers under contract to employers in Canada and approved by the Canadian government. Initially, immigration under the agreement was limited to 400 per year, not including the wives and children of residents of Canada. Later, the limit was reduced to 150 and changed to include all family members.

Vancouver Riot, 1907

The Asiatic Exclusion League fired up an already anti-Asian society and it all came to a head with the Vanvouver Riot in September 1907. A mob of about 9,000 white demonstrators attacked Vancouver's Chinatown and Japantown. The mayor and local police were slow to react, allowing the riot to continue longer than necessary. This photo shows the smashed windows of businesses in the downtown area. According to reports, the Japanese-Canadian merchants were the only ones to actively defend themselves. A Chinese-language newspaper in Taiwan claimed that Japanese-Canadian residents had killed four white men in the riot, although Vancouver papers reported no deaths.

"A mob of about 9,000 white demonstrators attacked Vancouver's Chinatown and Japantown."

WHITE IMMIGRATION

ORIENTAL EXCLUSION

B.C. IMMIGRATION

POLICY

Asians not welcome
This 1907 cartoon illustrates how the majority of white British Columbians felt about allowing immigration from Asia to continue. Notice how the Asian immigrants are pictured as animals, barely human, while the white immigrants are shown as highly civilized.

Aftermath of the riot
The day after the riot, Vancouver Asians went on a general strike and did not appear on the streets for several days. Police roped off the area that combined Chinatown and Japantown and held it under martial law for ten days. The military took over the area and the people living there had to obey orders, such as being off the streets after dark. The federal government appointed future Prime Minister William Lyon Mackenzie King to sort out what damages should be paid to the merchants who had their stores destroyed and looted. His final report recommended compensation of $23,421 to the larger Chinese community of Vancouver and $9,175 to the Japanese community of Vancouver, where sixty businesses had been damaged.

Racist Treatment

Racism toward Asian immigrants was expressed in British Columbia as early as 1858, when Chinese men flooded into BC to join the gold rush on the Fraser River. Thousands more arrived to work on the Canadian Pacific Railway from the East to Vancouver. When that work ended in 1885, many BC residents of European descent wanted the Asian-Canadian workers repatriated back to their homelands.

These views led the BC legislature to adopt a string of new laws intended to make working very difficult for those Asians who stayed. Workers of Japanese origin and descent were not allowed to join unions. The *Mining Safety Act* banned them from working underground. They were not allowed to work in forestry on Crown land. On the railways they were barred from higher-paid occupations, such as engineer, leaving them able to work only as lower-paid cooks or porters.

After a government Royal Commission on the BC fishery, called the Duff Commission, new laws stripped fishing licences from about half the Japanese-Canadian fishermen working in coastal waters.

Some Japanese Canadians got organized and fought these racist policies in public and through the courts. They didn't have much success.

Racist immigration policies

This 1903 political cartoon shows Prime Minister Laurier beating a Chinese man. Canada had just raised the Chinese Head Tax for immigrants to $500 from the original $50. Laurier is shown as wanting to avoid confrontation with the Japanese man because of Japan's military strength and their recent alliance with Great Britain. Canada was not as concerned about its relations with China at the time.

Calling on white males

This early-1900s sign in Vancouver invited white males to register for voting. By 1895, BC had taken the right to vote from all Asian Canadians. This left them without a voice to affect the racist laws that tried to push them out of work and out of the country.

A ctizen with no vote (opposite page)

Tomekichi Homma, pictured here, was a Vancouver boarding-house owner. In 1900, as a naturalized Canadian citizen, he applied to be added to the BC voter's list. His effort to fight for his rights was denied by the BC authorities, but a BC judge decided that the clause barring Asian Canadians from voting was beyond the powers of those authorities and that Homma should be granted the right to vote. That decision was overturned two years later by the Privy Council, at the time the supreme legal authority for Canada, and so Asian-Canadian citizens continued to be deprived by the legal system of the right to vote.

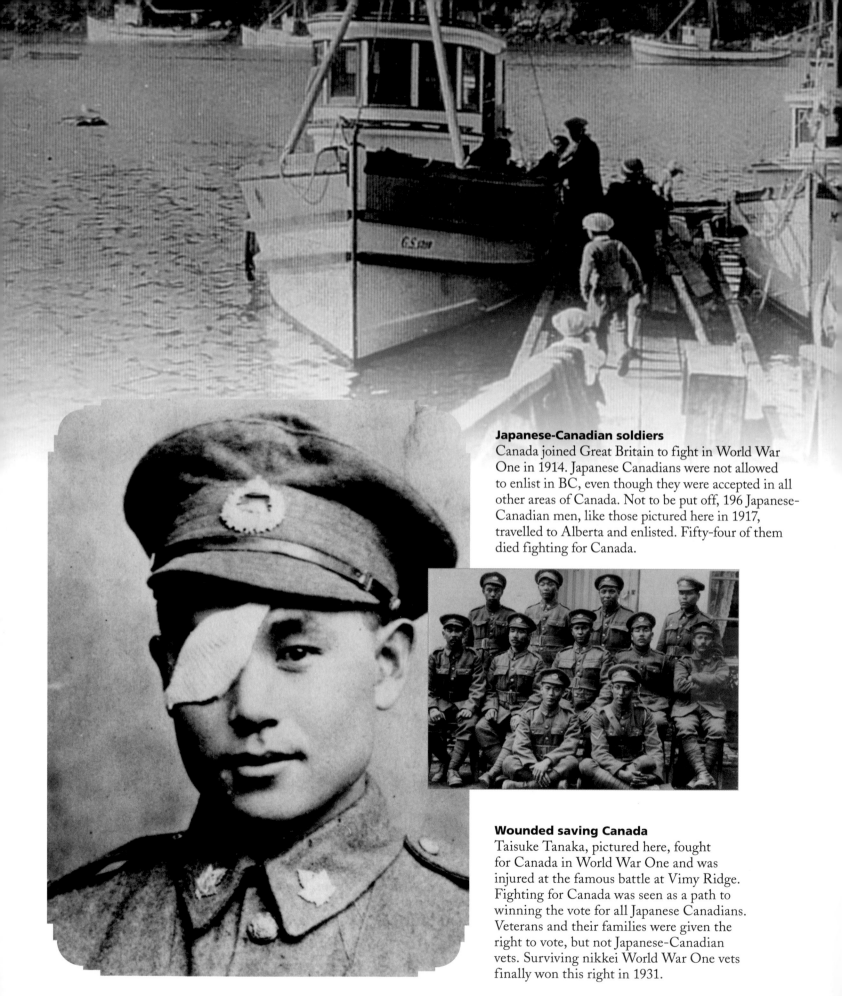

Japanese-Canadian soldiers

Canada joined Great Britain to fight in World War One in 1914. Japanese Canadians were not allowed to enlist in BC, even though they were accepted in all other areas of Canada. Not to be put off, 196 Japanese-Canadian men, like those pictured here in 1917, travelled to Alberta and enlisted. Fifty-four of them died fighting for Canada.

Wounded saving Canada

Taisuke Tanaka, pictured here, fought for Canada in World War One and was injured at the famous battle at Vimy Ridge. Fighting for Canada was seen as a path to winning the vote for all Japanese Canadians. Veterans and their families were given the right to vote, but not Japanese-Canadian vets. Surviving nikkei World War One vets finally won this right in 1931.

Anti-Japanese fishing policy

By 1920, Japanese Canadians owned nearly half of the fishing licences in BC. Protests from white and Aboriginal fishermen prompted the federal government to implement a series of policies in the 1920s. These laws ended up excluding about half of the Japanese-Canadian fishermen from BC's commercial fisheries. In addition, Japanese Canadians could get only certain licences, had to fish in specified districts, and were not allowed to use gasoline-powered boats. Fishermen who were white or Aboriginal had no restrictions. These racist policies severely limited the success of the Japanese-Canadian fishermen who remained in the industry. In 1928, they took their fight to the Supreme Court of Canada and won the battle to eliminate the restrictions on fishing licences and the restriction against using motorized fishing boats.

Fighting for their rights

The Japanese Canadian Citizens League was formed in 1936 to fight for full rights of citizenship. This delegation went to Ottawa in 1936 to get the vote for all Japanese Canadians. They were denied. Without the vote in BC, Asian Canadians were excluded from jobs in provincially licensed and controlled professions, such as law, medicine, and pharmacy.

> "Japanese Canadians were not allowed to enlist in BC even though they were accepted in all other areas of Canada."

Racial Segregation

British Columbia described itself as being a white society with high British standards and loyalty to king and country. The reality, however, is that it was a diverse multicultural society. BC was the true home of a large population of Aboriginal peoples who had been pushed off their lands by Europeans. It was also settled by Japanese, Chinese, and Sikh cultures that the British-Canadian elite preferred to ignore. The visible minorities were largely relegated to low-paying jobs and ghetto-like housing. Many non-white Canadians ended up in logging camps, cannery housing, and other resource-related communities, effectively segregated from the mainstream white society.

From majority to minority
Like all of Canada, the land that made up British Columbia was originally home to Aboriginal First Nations. When the Europeans arrived, First Nations peoples became an oppressed minority on their own lands.

Joining the workforce

Some Aboriginal people continued to follow their traditional lifestyle, while others ended up working for white employers. Many worked alongside other minorities in the resource industries. This First Nations woman is pictured working in a cannery in 1913.

"The visible minorities were largely relegated to low-paying jobs and ghetto-like housing."

No daycare

If a woman had young children, she often had to bring them to work with her. Here, a First Nations woman works in the Imperial Cannery, Steveston, in 1913, while her children wait for her.

Segregated housing

Housing supplied by the Imperial Cannery in Steveston, shown here in 1913, was not much better than a bunch of shacks. Aboriginal and immigrant workers were paid less than their white counterparts and lived in much poorer conditions. The housing was separated so that First Nations, Japanese, and Chinese workers were segregated into their own areas.

Descendants of slaves

Salt Spring Island, off the coast of BC, was home to a group of black families as early as the 1800s. Pictured here are descendants of Howard and Hannah Estes, a couple who had been slaves in Missouri. They bought their freedom and later moved to BC in 1859, where they settled into farming on Salt Spring.

"17,000 Chinese immigrants arrived in BC between 1881 and 1885"

English Bay's Joe Fortes

Joe Fortes, shown here in 1922, was one of the few black men in BC's Lower Mainland. He came to Canada from his native Barbados via England in 1885. The large, gentle man taught thousands of children to swim off the beach near his home on the shore of English Bay and became Vancouver's first official lifeguard in 1900. Today his name is carried by a popular Vancouver restaurant, a branch of the Vancouver Public Library, and a monument near the site of his home.

Building the CPR
These men were some of the 17,000 Chinese immigrants who arrived in BC between 1881 and 1885. Many ended up as labourers on the BC section of the Canadian Pacific Railway. They outnumbered non-Chinese labourers two to one.

East Indians came too
Immigration from India began when India was declared a British colony in 1857, making all its residents British subjects. This meant that Indians were free to live in any country of the British Empire, including Canada. These Sikhs, pictured here in 1907, worked in the forestry industry in BC.

Steveston

Steveston, on BC's Lower Mainland, was the centre of the BC salmon fishery. It had the second-highest population of Japanese Canadians in BC, after Japantown in Vancouver. Drawn to the canneries and fishing fleet, Japanese immigrants flocked to the town and settled in to work and raise their families there. The Dantai, started in 1897, was a Japanese community organization created primarily to protect fishermen's rights and fight racist policies. Its mandate also covered health care and education for Japanese Canadians. Because of the Dantai, the quality of life was greatly improved for the Japanese-Canadian citizens of Steveston.

From Wakayama to Steveston
These Japanese immigrants, photographed in Steveston in 1918, were from the Wakayama area of Japan. More Japanese immigrants came from Wakayama than from anywhere else in Japan, and most of them settled in Steveston.

Working at the canneries
The Gulf of Georgia Cannery, pictured here, employed a large number of Japanese immigrants and their families.

Hard at work
These Japanese-Canadian men are working inside the Scottish-Canadian Cannery in Steveston.

Japanese-Canadian businesses
Some Japanese Canadians opened their own shops to cater to the large nikkei population in Steveston. This is the Mukai Confectionery store in 1942.

" ...only children whose parents owned property could attend school."

Unfair treatment
Japanese-Canadian fishermen were paid lower wages and offered poorer housing than white men doing the same jobs. This picture shows some of the cannery housing in Steveston.

Segregation in school
In 1907, the Richmond School District, which included Steveston, decided that only children whose parents owned property could attend school. The majority of Japanese-Canadian families lived in company housing, so the Japanese Language School was opened in 1909 by the Dantai. The language of instruction was Japanese, but English was added as an extra class later on.

Starting young
The Dantai approached the United Church Women's Missionary Society to start a kindergarten in Steveston to teach English. Since the youngest Japanese-Canadian children spoke Japanese at home, it was hoped that English instruction in kindergarten would prepare them for entry into school. The 1927 graduating class is pictured here.

A seaside playground
With parents working in the canneries and cannery-supplied homes built on stilts over the water, many Japanese-Canadian children grew up playing on the wharves.

I scream, you scream...
It was a happy day in Steveston when these children got a special treat of ice cream, 1913.

"...the first medical insurance in Canada."

The Japanese Hospital
The original Japanese Hospital began treating Japanese Canadians in 1894, but in June 1900 a larger hospital was built by the Japanese-Canadian community. Families paid a fee of eight dollars per year for full medical coverage, for what some believe was the first medical insurance in Canada.

Sumo in Steveston
The Steveston Sumo club, pictured here in 1911, was popular with young Japanese-Canadian men.

Japanese Language School
This high-school graduating class is posed outside the Japanese Language School in Steveston in 1940.

Powell Street, Vancouver

Vancouver's Powell Street was at the heart of a thriving residential and business district in Vancouver in the 1920s and 1930s.

The land originally belonged to First Nations peoples. It was occupied by Europeans in the mid-1800s, and the Aboriginal population was soon outnumbered. When Japanese immigrants were hired by employers, sometimes replacing Aboriginal workers, they moved into the area. Large tracts of land were purchased by developers of European descent and the first churches and cultural institutions were built for the European community. By the late 1890s, these residents were moving away and the area's population became largely Japanese Canadian, along with some First Nations peoples and other cultural minorities.

In the centre of the area was Oppenheimer Park. The park became the home of a highly successful Japanese-Canadian baseball team.

Attractive architecture
The Sun Bun-Tamura Building on Powell Street was an imposing building. The ornate decorative features on top reflect its Japanese-Canadian ownership.

Successful Japanese-Canadian enterprises
The Tai Shodo Company, pictured here in 1927, was one of many retail shops on Powell Street owned by Japanese Canadians.

Anything and everything

Japantown was where Japanese Canadians went to do all kinds of business. There they shopped for groceries, flowers, jewellery, and other wares. They ate at the Japanese and Chinese restaurants, and attended Buddhist and Christian services. They had their shoes repaired, their clothes dry cleaned, their hair cut, and their educational, medical, dental, and financial needs looked after. But there were no lawyers, pharmacists, or morticians. In order to join these professions, one had to be on the voter's list. Those living in outlying areas came to Powell Street to celebrate Japanese holidays and festivals. There were many places for local Japanese Canadians to shop on Powell Street and purchase items that were imported directly from Japan. This is the inside of the Tai Shodo Company, pictured in 1927.

Championship team

Oppenheimer Park, bordered by Powell Street on one side, was home to the famous Japanese-Canadian Asahi baseball team. When the team was playing, everyone stopped to watch and cheer. It was a source of great pride in the community. The Asahi team won the coveted Pacific Northwest Baseball Championship for five straight years. They were inducted into the Canadian Baseball Hall of Fame in 2003 and the BC Sports Hall of Fame in 2005.

Sticking Together

Due to the concentration of Japanese-Canadian families in resource towns where the men found work, it was common for all-Japanese-Canadian clubs and sports teams to start up. Sometimes these groups were cultural, such as the kendo club. But some groups got together because the local white population did not welcome Japanese Canadians into their own institutions.

Oriental orphan home
The Japanese Methodist Church, founded in Vancouver in 1896, ran Victoria's "Oriental Home" for children of Japanese and Chinese immigrants who were in need of care. By the time Methodists, Congregationalists, and Presbyterians merged to form the United Church of Canada in 1925, it had attracted more Japanese Canadians than all the other Christian churches combined.

Church groups
This 1930 photo shows a Japanese-Canadian Anglican group in Prince Rupert, BC.

Lone scout

Shige Yoshida tried to join the local Chemainus, BC, Boy Scout troop but was not welcomed. Undaunted, he achieved the level of scoutmaster through correspondence and proceeded to form an all-nisei (second-generation Japanese Canadians) Scout troop. This 1938 picture shows Yoshida, in the centre of the middle row wearing his Scout uniform, and his troop.

"…it was common for all-Japanese-Canadian clubs and sports teams to start up."

Dance group

This all-Japanese-Canadian girls' dance group was photographed in Victoria in 1939 in Western clothes, but they also performed in traditional kimonos.

JAPANESE RUGBY TEAM 1930.
VANCOUVER B.C.

Y. KAWAME. H. IWASHITA. Y. YAGAI. S. SHIMIZU. K. MATSUHARA. T. HAGIWARA. Y. MASUNAGA. S. KA... S. WADA. S. UEDA. M. FUJII. S. KATANA.

Non-traditional sport

Rugby was introduced to Japanese universities in 1899. Although not a traditional Japanese sport, this team from 1930 in Vancouver was made up entirely of Japanese-Canadian boys.

剣道

"Canadians were unfamiliar with the Japanese sport of sumo wrestling."

Kendo club

Kendo is the Japanese martial art of sword-fighting, usually using bamboo or wooden shinai instead of real swords. This group of young men and boys belonged to the local kendo club in Ocean Falls, a company town on BC's west coast owned and operated by Pacific Mills. It housed the largest Japanese-Canadian community outside of Vancouver Island and the Lower Mainland.

Sumo wrestling

Canadians were unfamiliar with the Japanese sport of sumo wrestling when it became popular in the local Japanese-Canadian communities. This picture shows a sumo wrestling tournament in Woodfibre, BC.

A Visible Minority

While many Japanese Canadians were concentrated in communities like the fishing village of Steveston, BC, or the Powell Street community of Vancouver, some families lived in areas where they were one of few — or the only — residents of Japanese origin or descent. As a result, their children went to schools where they were a minority — a visible minority (though that term was not used at the time). Some Japanese Canadians felt their children should become as Canadian as possible. Other children lived a dual life; they felt Canadian at school and Japanese at home.

Mary Haraga:
"Like many nisei, we lived in two cultures — Canadian and Japanese — and we were comfortable in both. At school, we spoke English and sang 'Alouette,' 'Maple Leaf Forever,' and 'There'll Always Be an England.' We learned about our Japanese heritage more through osmosis than through explicit teaching from our parents. We spoke Japanese at home and sang Japanese children's songs such as 'Moshi Moshi Kame-yo.' We also celebrated New Year's Japanese style."

Breaking a trail
Chitose "Josi" Uchida, pictured third from the top, was the daughter of a pioneering family. Out of thirty-eight students in the University of British Columbia's first graduating class in 1916, Josi Uchida was the only Japanese Canadian. By 1942, UBC had registered seventy-two male and fourteen female Japanese-Canadian graduates.

Two of 100

In 1922, this graduating class from King George V High School in Vancouver had only two Japanese-Canadian boys (bottom left).

Making the team

There were many all-Japanese-Canadian sports teams and clubs, but some nisei (second-generation Japanese Canadians) who attended non-segregated schools ended up as the only players of Japanese descent on a team. Here you can see a lone Japanese-Canadian boy on his high-school rugby team at King George V High School in 1933. Athletic nisei might have had an easier time fitting in at school; however, they were often shunned at social events such as dances.

Japanese Culture

When the Japanese immigrated to Canada they brought their culture with them. The first generation of immigrants, the issei, continued to speak Japanese in their homes and with their friends, so many never learned English. Although some immigrants assimilated into the Canadian culture, many held on to their traditional lifestyles. This set them apart from most of society. Their foods, customs, and dress seemed strange to their Canadian neighbours. Since there were concentrations of Japanese people in areas like Steveston and around Powell Street in Vancouver, Japanese immigrants were able to continue celebrating their culture and passing it on to their children, the nisei. These second-generation Japanese Canadians added Canadian pursuits to their lives and reflected both Canadian and Japanese cultures.

March 3 is Girls' Day in Japan
This traditional doll shrine was part of the Girl's Day celebrations in March. It is part of the Langham Museum collection in Kaslo, BC.

Japanese artwork
This fan was made and decorated in Japan. As a fine example of the beauty of Japanese decorative art, it is a prized possession of a Japanese-Canadian family.

Traditional painting
Bamboo and birds are recurring themes in Japanese paintings like this one. It, along with the fan shown above, is on display at the Nikkei Memorial Internment Centre in New Denver, BC.

"Their foods, customs, and dress seemed strange to their Canadian neighbours."

"She told us that the carp was a symbol of strength because it swam against the current and boys were expected, like the carp, to face and overcome difficulties."

Making music
Looking a little like a xylophone, this homemade musical instrument is part of the collection of artifacts on display at Kaslo's Langham Museum. While the issei enjoyed playing Japanese songs on their record players, their children, the nisei, preferred to listen to swing on the radio.

Chapter 2: Japanese Canadians in BC, 1900–1939

May 5 is Boys' Day

Carp streamers like these fly over Japanese homes on Boys' Day every May. Akira Horii recalls his first Boys' Day at the internment camp in East Lillooet. "My brothers and I were waiting for Boys' Day, May 5th. My mother had packed the sturdy samurai dolls and I brought the carp streamers in my suitcase. She told us that the carp was a symbol of strength because it swam against the current and boys were expected, like the carp, to face and overcome difficulties."

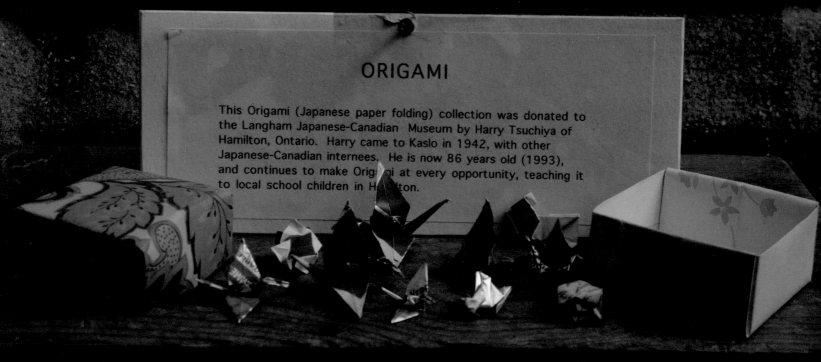

ORIGAMI

This Origami (Japanese paper folding) collection was donated to the Langham Japanese-Canadian Museum by Harry Tsuchiya of Hamilton, Ontario. Harry came to Kaslo in 1942, with other Japanese-Canadian internees. He is now 86 years old (1993), and continues to make Origami at every opportunity, teaching it to local school children in Hamilton.

The art of origami

Origami is the traditional Japanese art of paper folding. Often made with beautifully patterned, fine paper, origami shapes range from simple boxes to ornate figures of animals and people. These samples are now on display at the Langham Museum in Kaslo.

Language Schools

Education is very important to Japanese families. Early immigrants who could afford it sent their children back to Japan for schooling. The next best thing was to send them to Japanese-language schools in Canada where they would be with other Japanese kids and speak their parents' language. By 1939, more than sixty Japanese-language schools opened across BC. In 1919, the Vancouver Japanese Language School stopped teaching general subjects and began teaching only the Japanese language. Youngsters complained about having to attend Japanese-language school after public school and on weekends. However, not all Japanese parents felt it was important to retain the Japanese language and culture, and many nisei children attended local schools. The athletic students had a better chance of fitting in than most, as sports tended to eliminate cultural barriers.

Vancouver Japanese Language School
The largest Japanese-language school, pictured here in 1919, still exists today on Alexander Street in Vancouver. These students were free to attend local schools, but their parents chose a segregated Japanese-only school. The town of Chemainus and the Marpole district of Vancouver both attempted to keep Asian students out of the local schools, but failed to have this racist policy implemented.

Closed doors
Even if the students in this 1928 graduating class of the Vancouver Japanese Language School excelled in their studies and went on to university, they were most likely facing closed doors when it came to jobs. It was not illegal to discriminate by race when it came to hiring, and European-Canadian employers commonly refused to hire individuals with the best qualifications if they were of Japanese origin.

No school buses
These Japanese-Canadian children in Ucluelet had to take a ferry across the bay to get to school.

Japanese school
The Meiwa Gakuen Elementary School was located on Triumph Street in Vancouver. This 1930s photo shows the school building, which was actually the home of Mr. and Mrs. Aoki, who ran the school.

Japanese institutions
These schools and churches were all owned by the Japanese communities in BC.

"Youngsters complained about having to attend Japanese-language school after public school."

へ加を附寄の弗千五萬二のりよ側本日

Canada Goes to War

On September 10, 1939, Canada, as a loyal British dominion, followed Britain in declaring war on Germany. The war effort rallied all Canadians to do their part. Ads appeared everywhere for men and women to join the military. The public was asked to give financial support through Victory Bonds. Many manufacturing plants were converted to make ammunition and military equipment. Homemakers were told to avoid waste and recycle just about everything. Even though the battle did not occur on Canadian soil, everyone was expected to make sacrifices for the cause.

Shipping out
Thousands of Canadian troops left on ships from Halifax to join the fight in Europe.

Rallying for the troops
This crowd on West Hastings Street in Vancouver was part of a war bond drive in the 1940s. It urged Canadians to invest their money in government bonds to help finance Canada's military efforts overseas.

"The war effort rallied all Canadians."

Join up
Recruitment posters and signs were everywhere in the 1940s. Just under 1.1 million men and women signed up at recruitment offices across the country to take on full-time duty in the armed forces.

SHOULDER TO SHOULDER

CANADIAN WOMEN'S ARMY CORPS

"... the Canadian Women's Army Corps marches shoulder to shoulder with Canada's Active Army down the road that leads to victory. Releasing their brothers-in-arms from many vital military activities, members of this now-famous corps have proudly and efficiently taken up their duties as an integral part of the Canadian Army."

ADMINISTRATIVE · DRIVING · TECHNICAL · STOREWOMEN
AN INTEGRAL PART OF THE CANADIAN ARMY

Buy Victory Bonds

Since Canada had just come out of the Depression, finances were tight. Victory Bond campaigns inspired Canadians to lend their money to the government at low interest rates in support of the war effort. The eleven Victory Bond campaigns over the course of the war raised more than eight billion dollars in Canada.

Be prepared!
This window display in the Woodwards department store in Vancouver was put on by the Air Raid Precautions (ARP) team. They worked to educate the public about safety preparations they should have in place in their homes in case of a bombing raid, expected from Japan.

Practice makes perfect
The ARP team was responsible for ensuring the safety of all citizens and training them in the use of shelters and gas masks, and general wartime practices. Here, a group of students sit in their Vancouver classroom in the 1940s, wearing gas masks in an ARP training session.

"The eleven Victory Bond campaigns over the course of the war raised more than eight billion dollars in Canada."

We want your **KITCHEN WASTE**

PIG FOOD

KEEP IT DRY, FREE FROM GLASS, BONES, TINS.
IT ALSO FEEDS POULTRY. YOUR COUNCIL WILL COLL

Fighting from the kitchen

When it came to the war effort, no home was untouched. This poster is aimed at women, the main cooks in most households, and asks them to save their kitchen waste for pick-up and use as animal feed. Helping feed animals provided more food to be shipped overseas to the troops.

"War posters were a huge part of the propaganda campaign."

The propaganda campaign

War posters like this one were a huge part of the propaganda campaign launched by Canada's Wartime Information Board. More than 700 posters were produced throughout the war. This one tries to motivate workers to work harder and more efficiently to improve Canada's production and chances of winning the war.

"Every rivet we drive—every bolt we turn—every ounce we sweat, brings victory a little closer. Breaking production records is the Canadian way of doing things!"

PRODUCE FOR VICTORY!

So long, son
These Canadian troops were marching down 8th Street in New Westminster, BC, in 1939, heading off to war. A small boy reaches out to his father's hand, possibly for the last time.

Japanese Canadians Join the War Effort

When Canada joined Britain in declaring war on Germany, Japanese Canadians joined the war effort in many ways. Even schoolchildren joined their classmates in helping. Akira Horii remembers their contributions: "In September 1939, I was beginning the third grade at Lord Strathcona Elementary School when Canada and its allies entered the war. All the students became enthusiastically involved in many projects in support of Great Britain. In grade four, my class made a beautiful quilt and we proudly sent it to England."

Here, you are free!
Japanese Canadians bought $300,000 in Victory Bonds in support of Canadian troops. Note the words on the poster: "Free from confiscation, from suffering, from wanton imprisonment without cause."

HERE, YOU ARE FREE!

FREE to live and work in peace and comfort. Free to dream, free to plan your future. Free from cruel decrees. Free from confiscation, from suffering, from wanton imprisonment without cause.

Yes, you are FREE, in Canada. Keep it that way. Help to free Canada from a longer war, from further suffering, from greater trials. Hasten our Victory, speed the return of our troops!

Here is how you can do it. LEND YOUR MONEY TO CANADA. You will be given Victory Bonds as security, and every dollar will be repaid to you in FULL—with interest! This is Canada's promise to you, and Canada has always kept its promises to pay.

When you LEND your money for Victory Bonds, it is still your money. It earns good interest.

Every dollar you LEND enables Canada to give her troops more power, hastens their victory, brings the bright post-war period closer, and helps you to remain free.

LEND your money, now. Lend freely. Lend all you can out of savings, then lend more on the instalment plan. You will get Victory Bonds for every dollar you LEND, and every bond will be a protection for your own, and your family's future.

HOW TO BUY

Give your order to the Victory Loan salesman who calls on you or place it with any branch bank or trust company. You can also buy Bonds through your employer for cash or on the Payroll Savings Plan. Or send your order to your local Victory Loan Headquarters. Any one of these agencies will be glad to give you every assistance in completing your application. Bonds may be bought in denominations of $50, $100, $500, $1,000 and larger.

SPEED THE VICTORY

BUY VICTORY BONDS

NATIONAL WAR FINANCE COMMITTEE

"Even school-children joined their classmates in helping."

Salmon for the troops
Akira Horii's father was a successful fisherman. Akira recalled, "My father's fishing buddies in the Japanese Upper Fraser River Fishermen's Association sent three-and-a-quarter tons of canned salmon to Britain in support of the Allied cause."

We need you, except if you're Japanese
The military was desperate to sign up Canadians, both men and women. But in January 1941, Prime Minister Mackenzie King announced that anyone of Japanese ancestry was "exempted" from service. He really meant "excluded." This was a terrible blow to patriotic young nisei. When Japanese-Canadian men born in Canada tried to enlist at recruitment offices like the one pictured here, they were refused. Yoshiaki Sato, a five-year member of the 47th Westminster Regiment, tried to enlist. He argued: "After rapping us right and left about disloyalty, this so-called Canadian democracy owes us the chance to prove our loyalty." He was rejected.

Canada Goes to War Against Japan

In the months leading up to the bombing of Hawaii's Pearl Harbor in December 1941, Japan had attacked other countries in Southeast Asia. In Canada, public concern over Japan was growing. The federal government imposed compulsory registration of Japanese-Canadian males over the age of sixteen in early March 1941. The RCMP also "kept an eye on" the Japanese-Canadian community. Immediately following the Pearl Harbor attack, Canada declared war on Japan and invoked the *War Measures Act* to declare every Japanese Canadian — born here or not, a citizen of Canada or not, and even those who had served in the Canadian forces in World War One — an enemy alien. It was a very scary and confusing time for Japanese Canadians. Mickey Nakashima recalls, "The atmosphere of camaraderie and 'togetherness' changed in December 1941, when we heard on the radio that Japan had attacked Pearl Harbor. A dark gloom descended on our household. No one spoke. We didn't want to believe it to be true." When nisei students got to school the next day, they were in for an unpleasant surprise.

"A dark gloom descended."

Mary Haraga:
"I was in grade 7 at Mt. Lehman Superior School when Japan attacked Pearl Harbor. My grandfather, who had come to Canada in the late nineteenth century, had been following Japan's inroads into Asia on the radio and when he heard about the attack, he told the family that Japan was coming to amerika [America] to rescue us. He thought of himself as Japanese first. My parents were born in Japan but they viewed Canada as their home since both were in their teens when they arrived here. They were incredulous and fearful. I, on the other hand, did not give the news a second thought and dismissed their fears — 'It's only old people's talk. We're Canadian.'"

Mickey Nakashima:
"I was fourteen years old and attended a small, four-room school that went from grades one to twelve. My brothers and I were popular because we were good athletes and did well academically. Monday, December 8th, was hard at school. That morning when I approached, all conversation stopped and I knew what they had been discussing. I tried to act 'normal.' My classmates tried also. No one talked in front of me about the situation and gradually things went back to normal, but not really. The next day, the principal took aside the four nisei students and told us that she was sorry but we could no longer march with the cadets. We stood on the side forlornly as our classmates marched by."

Attack on Pearl Harbor
On December 7th, 1941, the Japanese Air Force attacked the American navy base at Pearl Harbor, Hawaii. These paintings show the sinking of the *Arizona*, an American battleship. The United States, which had refused to join the war in Europe, joined its allies in declaring war on Japan and the axis countries of Germany and Italy.

Mary Ohara:
"I was looking forward to the Christmas concert when news on the radio on December 7th changed our lives. I sensed that my parents were worried about possible consequences but I brushed it aside saying 'I'm Canadian.' However, when I arrived at school the next morning, I knew immediately that something was wrong. My friends looked away when I greeted them. They looked embarrassed. I soon learned that their parents had told them that they were not to socialize with the 'Japanese enemy.' My parents feared for our safety and would not allow us to walk the one hour to and from school, especially in the dark. I missed the Christmas concert."

Canada Goes to War Against Japan

"Canadian troops were in battle against Japan."

Canadian troops go to Hong Kong

Six weeks prior to Pearl Harbor, nearly 2,000 Canadian troops, like the ones pictured here, had been sent to Hong Kong to help the British defend its colony in case of attack by Japan. The attack came at the same time as the bombing of Pearl Harbor. Canadian troops were in battle against Japan.

Canadians at war
The Canadian contingent lands in Hong Kong, 1941.

WANT TO AVOID THIS?

Canadians become prisoners of war

More than 500 Canadians were wounded in the battle of Hong Kong, 290 were killed in the fight, and 264 died as prisoners of war (POWs). News of murder, unusual cruelty, and starvation of POWs at the hands of the Japanese increased the fear and hatred of Canadians for their Japanese-Canadian neighbours. These Canadian POWs in Hong Kong were among the survivors.

WANT TO AVOID THIS?

JAP.

CANADA

SUBSCRIBE TO CANADA'S SECOND VICTORY LOAN!

Spreading fear and loathing

When Canada declared war on Japan, the attack on Japanese Canadians at home also ramped up. This February 17, 1942 cartoon from the *Victoria Daily Times* is a clear message to the public — they must support Canada's war effort or fall victim to Japanese brutality. Bombarded with images like this in the media and racist comments by many BC politicians, the public began to equate the enemy abroad with the Japanese Canadians at home.

Japanese-Canadian Citizens Lose Their Rights

Although the RCMP had been registering all Japanese-Canadian males over sixteen years old since March 1941, the government's racist policies escalated following the Japanese attack on Pearl Harbor. Curfews were imposed, and "dangerous possessions" were confiscated. Of the more than 23,000 nikkei in Canada at the time, over 75 per cent were Canadian citizens. All were designated enemy aliens by government regulation. As enemy aliens, they had no rights to freedom, trial by jury, presumption of innocence, or other rights we take for granted today.

Notice to male enemy aliens

Once the *War Measures Act* was invoked, all people of Japanese descent were labelled enemy aliens. An official poster from February 7, 1942 tells all male Japanese Canadians eighteen to forty-five years old to leave a 100-mile-wide "secure zone" along the west coast of BC.

NOTICE TO ALL
MALES
OF JAPANESE RACIAL ORIGIN

Every MALE person, 18 years of age or over, of Japanese racial origin now in the district or vicinity of the cities of Vancouver, New Westminster, North Vancouver and the towns of West Vancouver and Steveston must report at the Royal Canadian Mounted Police Barracks at 33rd Avenue and Heather Street, Vancouver, B. C., between the hours of 9:00 a.m. and 12:00 noon as follows:

JAPANESE NATIONALS......March 27, 1942
NATURALIZED
CANADIANS ....March 30, 1942
CANADIAN BORN ....March 31, 1942

Unless in possession of a permit to remain in the defense area issued by the British Columbia Security Commission. Failure to comply with this order will entail a penalty of five hundred dollars fine ($500.00) and one year imprisonment.

By order:
AUSTIN C. TAYLOR,
Chairman,
B. C. Security Commission

Mary Haraga:

"I celebrated my 'sweet sixteenth' birthday by reporting to the RCMP office. There I was fingerprinted, photographed, and issued an 'alien' registration number. My card bore the stamp 'Canadian born.' It was a confusing time. For me, the worst part was being declared an enemy alien by my own country. I was a patriotic Canadian but I had the face of the enemy. It was the first time in my life that I had felt rejected."

Receipt for gun seizure
All firearms owned by Japanese Canadians were seized by the authorities. This receipt records the confiscation of two "ancient shotguns."

NOTICE

TO ALL PERSONS OF JAPANESE RACIAL ORIGIN

Having reference to the Protected Area of British Columbia as described in an Extra of the Canada Gazette, No. 174 dated Ottawa, Monday, February 2, 1942:-

EVERY PERSON OF THE JAPANESE RACE, WHILE WITHIN THE PROTECTED AREA AFORESAID, SHALL HEREAFTER BE AT HIS USUAL PLACE OF RESIDENCE EACH DAY BEFORE SUNSET AND SHALL REMAIN THEREIN UNTIL SUNRISE ON THE FOLLOWING DAY, AND NO SUCH PERSON SHALL GO OUT HIS USUAL PLACE OF RESIDENCE AFORESAID UPON THE STREETS OR OTHERWISE DURING THE HOURS BETWEEN SUNSET AND SUNRISE;

NO PERSON OF THE JAPANESE RACE SHALL HAVE IN HIS POSSESSION OR USE IN SUCH PROTECTED AREA ANY MOTOR VEHICLE, CAMERA, RADIO TRANSMITTER, RADIO RECEIVING SET, FIREARM, AMMUNITION OR EXPLOSIVE;

IT SHALL BE THE DUTY OF EVERY PERSON OF THE JAPANESE RACE HAVING IN HIS POSSESSION OR UPON HIS PREMISES ANY ARTICLE MENTIONED IN THE NEXT PRECEDING PARAGRAPH, FORTHWITH TO CAUSE SUCH ARTICLE TO BE DELIVERED UP TO ANY JUSTICE OF THE PEACE RESIDING IN OR NEAR THE LOCALITY WHERE ANY SUCH ARTICLE IS HAD IN POSSESSION, OR TO AN OFFICER OR CONSTABLE OF THE POLICE FORCE OF THE PROVINCE OR CITY IN OR NEAR SUCH LOCALITY OR TO AN OFFICER OR CONSTABLE OF THE ROYAL CANADIAN MOUNTED POLICE.

ANY JUSTICE OF THE PEACE OR OFFICER OR CONSTABLE RECEIVING ANY ARTICLE MENTIONED IN PARAGRAPH 2 OF THIS ORDER SHALL GIVE TO THE PERSON DELIVERING THE SAME A RECEIPT THEREFOR AND SHALL REPORT THE FACT TO THE COMMISSIONER OF THE ROYAL CANADIAN MOUNTED POLICE, AND SHALL RETAIN OR OTHERWISE DISPOSE OF ANY SUCH ARTICLE AS DIRECTED BY THE SAID COMMISSIONER.

ANY PEACE OFFICER OR ANY OFFICER OR CONSTABLE OF THE ROYAL CANADIAN MOUNTED POLICE HAVING POWER TO ACT AS SUCH PEACE OFFICER OR OFFICER OR CONSTABLE IN THE SAID PROTECTED AREA, IS AUTHORIZED TO SEARCH WITHOUT WARRANT THE PREMISES OR ANY PLACE OCCUPIED OR BELIEVED TO BE OCCUPIED BY ANY PERSON OF THE JAPANESE RACE REASONABLY SUSPECTED OF HAVING IN HIS POSSESSION OR UPON HIS PREMISES ANY ARTICLE MENTIONED IN PARAGRAPH 2 OF THIS ORDER, AND TO SEIZE ANY SUCH ARTICLE FOUND ON SUCH PREMISES;

EVERY PERSON OF THE JAPANESE RACE SHALL LEAVE THE PROTECTED AREA AFORESAID FORTHWITH;

NO PERSON OF THE JAPANESE RACE SHALL ENTER SUCH PROTECTED AREA EXCEPT UNDER PERMIT ISSUED BY THE ROYAL CANADIAN MOUNTED POLICE;

IN THIS ORDER, "PERSONS OF THE JAPANESE RACE" MEANS, AS WELL AS ANY PERSON WHOLLY OF THE JAPANESE RACE. A PERSON NOT WHOLLY OF THE JAPANESE RACE IF HIS FATHER OR MOTHER IS OF THE JAPANESE RACE AND IF THE COMMISSIONER OF THE ROYAL CANADIAN MOUNTED POLICE BY NOTICE IN WRITING HAS REQUIRED OR REQUIRES HIM TO REGISTER PURSUANT TO ORDER-IN-COUNCIL P.C. 9760 OF DECEMBER 16th, 1941.

DATED AT OTTAWA THIS 26th DAY OF FEBRUARY, 1942.

To be posted in a Conspicuous

Curfew imposed
This 1942 notice to "all people of Japanese racial origin" warned of a new curfew that had been imposed, as well as the government seizure of personal possessions.

Registration for all
Right after Canada declared war on Japan, all Japanese citizens sixteen or older and those who became Canadian citizens after 1922 had to register with the Registrar of Enemy Aliens. Two months later, the registration was extended to everyone of "Japanese racial origin," regardless of their citizenship.

Akira Horii:
"Japantown came to a standstill bringing with it economic hardship and a halt to social life. There were no late ball games, judo practices, concerts, or visiting; no 'hanging out' by the young nisei or listening and dancing to jukeboxes at a café. We were warned that breaking the curfew could lead to severe punishment, including being sent to a prisoner-of-war camp in a place no one had heard of — Angler, Ontario."

Radios were taken away
Radios, like this one now in the New Denver Nikkei Internment Memorial Centre, and cameras were confiscated from all Japanese families beginning in February 1942.

Japanese-Canadian Citizens Lose Their Rights

Normal Life Comes to a Halt

The day after the Pearl Harbor attack, the *War Measures Act* was invoked, and the lives of more than 21,000 Japanese Canadians were changed forever. Many lost their jobs, their fishing boats were seized, and Japanese-Canadian cultural institutions and newspapers were closed. School children were shunned by their playmates of the day before. Japanese-language lessons were stopped, social life ended for teenagers, university students couldn't continue with their studies, and community gatherings ceased. Some were called racist names they had never heard. Akira Horii was in fifth grade when he heard the news about Pearl Harbor. "The local newspapers and radio stations kept repeating that there were Japanese spies ready to help the enemy when they invaded us. The *Vancouver Sun* said that… 'nobody could separate the sheep from the goats. We are in a war and the only safety lies in our adopting the totalitarian methods of the totalitarian countries of our enemies.'"

Royal Canadian Navy on-board

Here, a member of the Royal Canadian Navy seizes a Japanese fishing boat. Akira Horii's father, Ryotaro, had just had a new boat built at the beginning of the war in Europe, but it was seized by the government and later sold.

"1,200 Japanese fishing boats were seized"

Japanese-language schools closed

Japanese-language schools, like this one in Cumberland, were immediately shut down.

Japanese fishing boats seized (opposite page)

On December 8, 1941, 1,200 Japanese fishing boats were seized from their owners by the government. The authorities feared that the boats could be used by spies or those loyal to Japan to contact offshore Japanese military. There was no evidence whatsoever for these fears — not at the time, and not subsequently.

10,596 employees of the Canadian Pacific

The Canadian Pacific is proud of the fact that at May 15th, 1942, leave of absence had been granted to 10,596 employees from all branches of the Company, for active service in the Army, Navy, Air Force and for war service under direction of the British Admiralty

Proud of their patriotism
This Canadian Pacific Railway poster proudly states the number of its employees enlisted to fight in World War Two. However, it makes no mention of the number of faithful employees who were fired simply for being of Japanese descent.

Fired!
These Japanese-Canadian porters who worked for the CPR were immediately fired after Pearl Harbor. Many other industries also fired their Japanese-Canadian employees, causing great financial hardship within the community.

"The light on the memorial was turned out."

Lights out
In Vancouver's Stanley Park, a war memorial commemorates the Japanese-Canadian veterans of the First World War. Following Pearl Harbor, the light on the memorial was turned out, showing extreme disrespect to men who had fought for Canada.

The New Canadian

Early Japanese immigrants to Canada could read and write only in Japanese. Beginning in 1896, a weekly Japanese-language bulletin was published by the Vancouver Japanese Methodist Church to warn readers of anti-Japanese attitudes in local communities. In 1907, this became the first Japanese-language daily paper, *Canada Shimpo*. Other Japanese-language newspapers followed and in 1938 the first English-language Japanese-Canadian newspaper, the *New Canadian*, began publication. It was aimed at keeping up the morale of Canadian nisei, the children of the Japanese immigrants. The newspaper encouraged nisei to persevere in achieving their goals in Canada despite the hardships. It also spoke up for their rights and supported their fight for equality. The *New Canadian* was against all racism, regardless of the ethnicity of the people it was aimed at. Before Canada's declaration of war on Japan, the newspaper was produced from its offices in Vancouver as an English-only paper.

Following the attack on Pearl Harbor in 1941, the three Japanese-language newspapers were shut down by the government. The *New Canadian* was allowed to continue but its content was censored. The Canadian government used it to inform the Japanese-Canadian population about new rules and policies, such as curfews and evacuations, and other restrictions. With the closure of all Japanese-language newspapers, the government realized that their directives were not reaching the issei, or first-generation immigrants; a Japanese editor was hired and a new Japanese-language section added to the *New Canadian*.

The *New Canadian* became an important link between members of the widely dispersed Japanese-Canadian population. It kept people in touch with each other. Readers could get news of friends and family in other internment camps. The newspaper was a lifeline for many during the internment years and afterward.

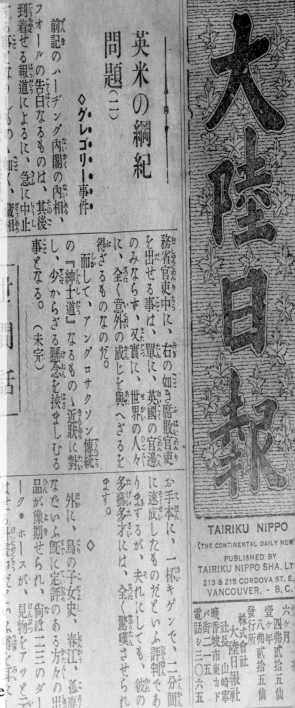

One of the first Japanese-language newspapers
The *Tairiku Nippo* was a mainstream Japanese-language newspaper. It was begun in BC in the early 1900s by Etsu Suzuki, an established journalist who had immigrated to Canada from Japan. In 1924 he left that paper to start a socialist paper called the *Minshu*.

EXTRA!

The New Canadian
THE VOICE OF THE SECOND GENERATION
Vol. V, No. 24 [A]   VANCOUVER, B. C.   THURS., FEB. 26, 1942

號
外

Ottawa Orders Dusk To Dawn Curfew

Not Yet Confirmed Here

Order to Remain in Homes
To Be Worked Out Soon

VANCOUVER, Feb. 26—The Canadian Press this
[...] carried an Ottawa dispatch saying that all Japan-
[...] Protected Area must
[...] and sunrise, under

夜間外出
禁止令
日没より日出迄

Two languages

This 1942 edition of the *New Canadian* told its readers
about the new curfew that was being imposed on them.
Notice the two languages — English and Japanese —
written side-by-side so that both issei and nisei could
understand the government's new orders.

Staff forced to leave the coast

After the attack on Pearl Harbor, when Japanese Canadians
were evacuated from the coast, the *New Canadian* and its
editors were forced to move from Vancouver to Kaslo, BC,
where they published the newspaper until the end of the war.
Censors forbade the paper from criticizing the government and
government policies. Editors had to walk a fine line between
supporting the civil rights of their readers and being used as a
voice of the government that was oppressing them. This picture
shows the staff in 1943.

Tom Shoyama, editor

Tom Shoyama, a graduate of UBC, became the editor of the
New Canadian in 1939 and remained until 1945, when he was
recruited for the Canadian armed forces. He is pictured here
in Kaslo, BC, in 1944. In later years Shoyama reflected on his
wartime role at the paper: "Our people were filled with such
great feelings of fear, dread, bitterness, anger, and resentment.
And we all wondered what the future held for us. To try to create
some stability and to try to fill in that huge gap of the unknown
was the role of our newspaper."

Working the linotype machine

Junji Ikeno operated the linotype machine, which printed the
words onto the paper. He is shown here in the Kaslo publishing
office in 1944.

Another move eastward

In 1945, the *New Canadian* and its staff left Kaslo and moved
east to Winnipeg. Pictured here from left to right are Harold
T. Mayeda, Rev. K. Shimizu, Junji Ikeno, editor Kasey Oyama,
E. C. Banno, Japanese-language editor Takaichi Umezuki, and
assistant editor Noji Murase. The *New Canadian* eventually
moved to Toronto and ceased publication in 1985.

The Decision to Intern

Japanese Canadians were banned from living within 100 miles (160 km) of Canada's west coast. Their boats, radios, and cameras were taken away, as were basically all their civil rights. But for some, that wasn't enough. Politicians in British Columbia, headed by MP Ian Mackenzie, campaigned to have all people of Japanese descent interned — removed from their homes and held separate from the rest of the population. The government in Ottawa didn't believe it was necessary. A meeting held by the Department of External Affairs revealed that both the RCMP and the military representatives agreed that Japanese Canadians did not pose any problem. Still, Mackenzie fought on and eventually convinced Ottawa to impose internment in BC.

Pushy politicians
British Columbia MP Ian Mackenzie, pictured here, led a BC delegation of Liberal and Conservative politicians to Ottawa, where he demanded the removal of Japanese-Canadian men from the coast. He lied about receiving hundreds of letters from the public that supported his demands. In reality, only a few letters were received, and some supported the Japanese Canadians.

HOW DO YOU TELL A JAP FROM A JAP?

Who's who?
The *Vancouver Sun* printed this cartoon in June 1943. It plays on the fears of those who believed it was impossible to separate Japanese Canadians who were loyal to Japan from those that were loyal to Canada.

Prime minister played politics

Prime Minister Mackenzie King, seen here, did not believe that Japanese Canadians were a security risk. If he followed the advice of his senior civil servants and military advisors, the internment would never have happened. Mackenzie King saw that internment could help his party's popularity in BC and help him gain support for his policy on conscription. He didn't care about the consequences for the Japanese-Canadian minority or the terrible injustice he was committing.

Keenleyside opposed internment

Highly ranked civil servants, such as Hugh Keenleyside at External Affairs, pictured here, opposed internment. But Ian Mackenzie pressed to have all male Japanese-Canadian citizens removed from the coast. And he didn't stop there. In the end, Prime Minister Mackenzie King decided to remove all Japanese Canadians, alien and naturalized, from the coast.

Top military were ignored

Like Ian Mackenzie, Major General R. O. Alexander was based in BC and held racist views about Japanese Canadians. He supported Mackenzie's fight for the internment of all Japanese Canadians, despite the fact that Ottawa's top military authorities felt that they were not a security risk. The head of the military in Ottawa refused to allow military personnel to be used for the roundup of Japanese Canadians in BC.

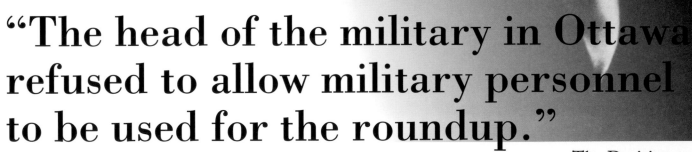

"The head of the military in Ottawa refused to allow military personnel to be used for the roundup."

Forced Removal

In early 1942, the Canadian government ordered Japanese-Canadian families to pack up their homes and leave them in the care of the Custodian of Enemy Alien Property. Families were forced to evacuate the BC coast and could take only what they could carry. Since many of the men had already been taken away to road camps, it was mainly women and children who were being evacuated.

Mary Haraga:

"When orders came for our family to relocate, my parents co-operated and obeyed. We stored our keepsakes: photo albums, letters, and mementos in trunks and boxes and lugged them upstairs to the attic. We carefully wrapped our best dishes and placed them in the walls of our farmhouse to protect them from breakage and looting. My father said that it was safer than burying them under a tree as our neighbours had done."

Get out!
This notice of evacuation ordered the Higashi family to report to Hastings Park Clearing Station. They were given three days' notice.

NOTICE No. 619

You are hereby ordered by the British Columbia Security Commission to report at Hastings Park Clearing Station, Vancouver, B.C., on the _____ day of _____, 1942, at 9:00 a.m., for the purpose of being evacuated from the Protected Area of British Columbia.

AUSTIN C. TAYLOR,

Chairman,

British Columbia Security Commission.

Handed to HIGASHI Masakazu No. _____
            NAME   Serial Number

on April 22nd, 1942

by _____
    Constable, R.C.M.P.

BRING BAGGAGE
LIMIT 30 LBS. HAND
100 LBS. HEAVY

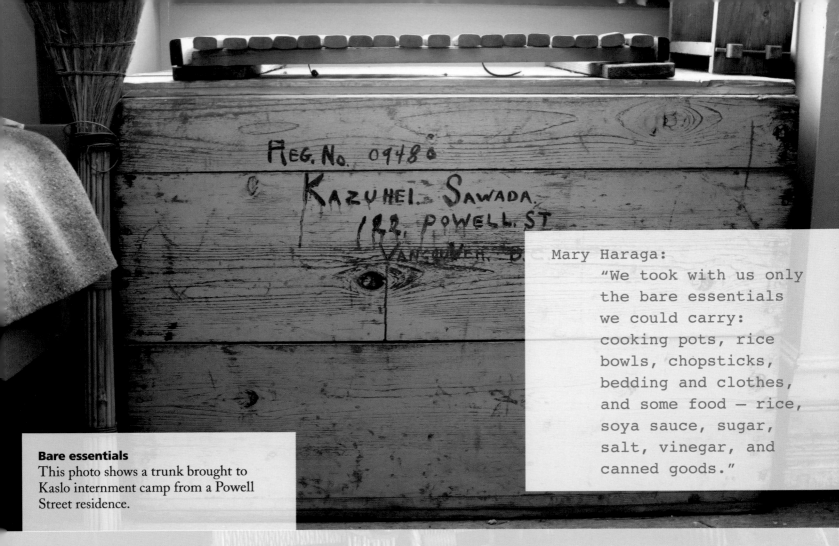

Bare essentials
This photo shows a trunk brought to Kaslo internment camp from a Powell Street residence.

Mary Haraga:
"We took with us only the bare essentials we could carry: cooking pots, rice bowls, chopsticks, bedding and clothes, and some food — rice, soya sauce, sugar, salt, vinegar, and canned goods."

Mary Ohara:
"I wanted to take my one and only doll but my mother said there was only space for necessities such as dishes, pots, pans, and bedding so I hid her in the corner of the attic and promised to come back for her soon. It was not to be."

Take it or leave it
Adults were restricted to 150 pounds (68 kg) of belongings, while children were allowed 75 pounds (34 kg) each. A variety of luggage that belonged to internees at the camp in New Denver is now displayed at the Nikkei Internment Memorial Centre there.

Mary Haraga:

"At thirteen years old, I was going on the train for the first time. It was so exciting. I guess I was caught up by the thrill of a new adventure so it did not occur to me to wonder why we were leaving or where we were going or why my father was not coming with us."

Next stop: internment camp
Many families boarded trains that took them either directly to an internment camp or, like this train, to the central holding facility, Hastings Park, in Vancouver. Later they were dispatched to the camps.

Deserted streets

Steveston, once full of Japanese-Canadian fishermen and their families, was emptied during the evacuation.

Closed forever

When the Japanese Canadians were evacuated, their businesses were left empty. Powell Street, shown here, once the heart of Japantown, was left deserted.

Women and Children Held in Livestock Stables

Once the decision to intern the Japanese Canadians was made, the BC Security Commission (BCSC) needed a place to send them while their ultimate destinations were organized. Hastings Park, the home of the Pacific National Exhibition in Vancouver, was chosen for its space and relative security. Thousands of Japanese Canadians were housed in the Exhibition's livestock stables and other buildings while they waited to be sent "away." Mary Ohara and June Fujiyama were among the crowds of internees that had to endure the appalling conditions at Hastings Park.

Mattresses for internees
In this photo, soldiers are busy stuffing straw into mattresses that will end up on crude metal bunk beds for the internees. As Mary Ohara recalls, "when the straw was new, it smelled fresh but as it got damp and mouldy, bedbugs infested our bedding."

Mary Ohara:

"We were herded in like animals. I was careful not to step on the excrement that had dried on the concrete. I felt sick from the stench so I climbed as quickly as I could onto the top bunk for some air. From there I saw the hundreds of other families moving into the stalls. Overhead were swallows. They had made their homes in the rafters and were swooping down quite close to the bunks. That night and every night thereafter, I checked my bunk before I climbed in for the night."

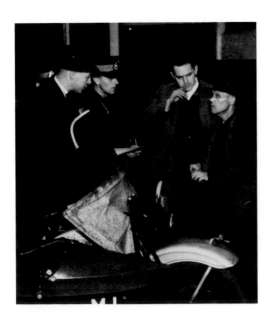

Under guard
The prison-camp nature of the confinement of everyone of Japanese ancestry is evident in this photo of an elderly Japanese-born Canadian resident. The atmosphere was intimidating and humiliating. Many thought that they would be detained only briefly and then be allowed to go back home.

June Fujiyama:

"What a shock to arrive and find the Park surrounded by a high barbed-wire fence and guarded by soldiers who were dressed in khaki and carrying guns. I was incredulous. 'Those guns are for us?'"

A sea of beds
The men and boys over twelve years old were separated from the women and children and sent to different buildings. This photo shows the rows of cots where the men were expected to sleep.

Separate dining halls
The men's dining hall, shown here, was set up in a former industrial building. The men were kept separate from the women and children. Used to a diet with a lot of fresh vegetables, Mary Ohara remembers eating a lot of bologna at Hastings Park. "Mothers of small children were worried because there was no fresh milk." Notice the little boy who sits by himself on the far right of the photo. His father had been sent to a road camp and his mother and sister were in the livestock building. He had nobody to look after him. He got the mumps during his stay at Hastings Park but his mother was not allowed to visit him. There were also times when there were no meals.

"Mothers of small children were worried because there was no fresh milk."

Working for the "other side"
Japanese-Canadian internees were recruited to work at Hastings Park, for kitchen and dining hall duties, seen here, and administrative jobs. For some, the jobs relieved boredom and provided a small income. June Fujiyama was hired in the office of the BC Security Commission.

June Fujiyama:
"Some nisei felt uncomfortable working for the BCSC because they were called 'inu' or dogs, meaning traitors for helping the government with its inhumane policies."

Women and Children Held in Livestock Stables

Crude conditions

This cement washing room was shared by thousands of women and children. There were only ten showers for about 1,500 women.

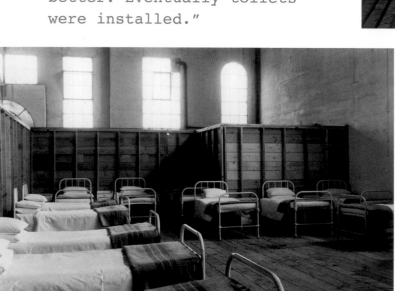

Mary Ohara:

> "They were made of animal drinking troughs — metal, with no seats or partitions. We were scared that we might fall in. The mothers stacked wooden apple boxes in front of the troughs so we could balance better. Eventually toilets were installed."

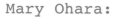

Sick and scared
Staying healthy was difficult in such dreadful conditions. The "hospital" pictured here was in a former livestock building.

Mary Ohara:

> "People came down with dysentery and diarrhoea. Mumps and other contagious diseases spread like wildfire in the cramped quarters. In about the third month, I contracted mumps and had to be isolated but there was no space available in the 'hospital.' An underground storage area for coal and animal feed was emptied and I was placed in 'the dungeon' with some other children. The younger ones were scared and screamed for their mothers day and night. Going to the toilet was a nightmare and the parents begged for large tin cans from the kitchen to use as bedpans. I tried to soothe them as best I could."

School must go on
Despite the incredible upheaval of being forced from their homes and kept like prisoners under such poor conditions, parents strived to organize schooling for the children. Here a high-school class concentrates on their work in a small room under the eaves of a former industrial building.

Property Seizure

Immediately after war was declared on Japan, all fishing boats belonging to Japanese Canadians were seized, leaving many without a means to make their living. As the evacuation proceeded, cars were impounded. Land, homes and their contents, businesses, and any other possessions that could not be carried in a few suitcases or trunks were transferred to the Custodian of Enemy Alien Property. In addition, Japanese-Canadian community-owned properties, such as churches, temples, language schools, co-operatives, and the hospital in Steveston, were also seized. Initially, it was the job of the Custodian to take charge of the properties until they could be returned to their original owners. In January 1943, everything changed. An order-in-council was approved by the Canadian government requiring all the property to be sold. This came as a total shock to the Japanese Canadians. Mary Haraga recalls, "My parents believed the government when it said that their farms, equipment, homes, and possessions would be held 'in trust.' They did not imagine that once they were incarcerated, what had taken them a lifetime to build would all be sold or auctioned off."

Mary Haraga:

"Later we found out that soon after we had been taken away, our house was torn down and our 40-acre farm became part of a military air base for the war effort. Other Japanese farms were sold to veterans and some were bought by Mennonite farmers."

Farms for sale

Mary Haraga grew up on a strawberry farm like the one pictured here. Her family believed they would go back to their farm once the war was over.

Cars seized

Japanese Canadians had already been stripped of their fishing boats, cameras, radios, and binoculars. Next, their cars were taken. In this 1942 photo, a Japanese-Canadian man is having his car seized by authorities.

"Churches, temples, and language schools were also seized."

Seized cars in Vancouver

Rows of cars seized from their Japanese-Canadian owners could be seen at the holding camp where people were required to report.

Lock, stock, and piano

Her piano was Mickey Nakashima's pride and joy before the war. Their possessions and property were all taken or sold off while the family toiled in the fields of Alberta.

"Many treasures were looted from empty homes."

Mickey Nakashima:
"When orders arrived for us to leave, we stored our best dishes, heirloom items, furniture, and my piano in one room and boarded up the house. We all believed that we would return soon."

A cruel system

Japanese-Canadian-owned properties, like this store, were sold off for prices far below fair market value. The proceeds of the sale were kept by the Custodian of Enemy Alien Property. The money was held in an account under the former owner's name and no interest was paid. Families could not draw more than $100 per month from their account. Families were expected to use all their savings to support themselves while in internment. If a family had cash in their account, they were not allowed to work in the camps. It was a cruel system that made an internee pay for his own internment, using proceeds from the unauthorized sale of his possessions.

Many motives (opposite page)

The Inouye family, pictured here in their parlour in the early 1900s, lost everything too. The Canadian government gained many things from the cruel policy of selling off the property of internees. It provided cheap land for returning war veterans. In some cases, the government was taking away land from Japanese-Canadian war veterans and giving it to European-Canadian vets. The proceeds were used to help pay for the internee's expenses while in the camps, saving the government some money. And, since it deprived internees of homes to return to, it discouraged Japanese Canadians from resettling in BC. As property sales continued, some Japanese families opted to leave the internment camps for eastern Canada where they could be free to start again.

Family heirlooms gone

This display of fine china, art, and ceremonial dolls at the Greenwood Museum is just a small sample of the valued articles that Japanese-Canadian internees left behind for safekeeping when they were rounded up. Children had to leave behind special belongings that would have given them joy and comfort, including toys, dolls, and books. Some neighbours were true friends to the Japanese Canadians and held on to their prized possessions while they were away. But many treasures were looted from empty homes even before the government sold off the rest to local bargain hunters. When Mickey Nakashima was living in Montreal after the war, she told a new friend about what had happened. "I complimented my friend on the beautiful china she had used to serve the lunch. She said that they belonged to her grandmother. I told her how lucky she was to have them and how my family heirlooms disappeared from our farmhouse in Mission. I had nothing that belonged to my grandmother or my mother. My friend cried when she heard my story."

CHAPTER 5
INTERNMENT AND FORCED LABOUR

Internment Camps

Women and children were sent to a variety of places including hastily built camps and old mining ghost towns transformed into camps. Most were separated from husbands and fathers, who were sent to work in road camps. The camps were designated for specific religions, such as Catholic, Anglican, and Buddhist. The BC government refused to pay for education, but the federal government eventually agreed to pay for schooling up to grade eight. Nisei tutors taught lessons to older students during the evenings and weekends, after finishing their day jobs. After that, the various churches set up high schools for Japanese-Canadian teens. Families who could afford it could apply to go to one of six self-supporting camps. Akira Horii's father was granted permission to stay with his family and move to a self-supporting camp in East Lillooet. He had to pay for the family's transportation and housing materials. Also, internees at self-supporting camps were responsible for building the school and paying the teachers' wages. Wherever they ended up, Japanese Canadians experienced harsh living conditions, loss of dignity, and loss of freedom.

> "Japanese Canadians experienced harsh living conditions, loss of dignity, and loss of freedom."

Arriving at Kaslo
Approximately 1,100 Japanese Canadians were sent to Kaslo, BC, a ghost town. This photo shows internees arriving on the waterfront in Kaslo in 1942. Seventy-eight people lived in the Langham building, which today is a museum with a permanent exhibition of the internment years.

Tents for internees
Some internees arrived at their destinations to find that the housing wasn't built yet. They had to live in tents, like these ones in Slocan, while they waited for the rough wooden buildings to go up.

No room
Crowded conditions were common. Canadians today can see how internees lived from places preserved from the internment, like this bedroom in a museum in Kaslo.

Internment shacks

For many families, a building like this one was what awaited them at the end of their long trip. Akira Horii remembers their newly built tarpapered shack in East Lillooet. "Built of green lumber, as the wood shrank cracks appeared between the boards. My brothers and I stuffed newspapers into the cracks but they didn't keep out the blistering heat in the summer or the cold in the winter." For most families, the accommodation in the internment camps was a far cry from the houses they had lived in before the internment.

"My brothers and I stuffed newspapers into the cracks but they didn't keep out the blistering heat in the summer or the cold in the winter."

The harsh climate

Coming from the BC coast, where weather is relatively mild, many internees were not prepared for harsh winter weather. They had a hard time dealing with the cold and snow, as seen in this photo of Tashme internment camp. Sandon, located in the mountains near Slocan, suffered severe winters and was known as "Camp Hell-Hole." It was the first camp to close and most of its 953 internees were transferred to New Denver.

Some fun

Despite the harsh conditions, families worked hard to resume some form of normal life in the camps. Schools, clubs, and events were organized for the children. These majorettes are performing for fellow internees at Tashme camp in 1945.

After-school crafts

Keeping children busy and happy during internment was sometimes difficult. At the camp in Kaslo, a wood-craft class was offered after school and children made these decorative pieces.

Chapter 5: Internment and Forced Labour

Missing fathers

With their husbands forced to go to the road camps, many mothers had a hard time providing for their youngsters alone. Lack of plumbing and heating made everything more difficult and uncomfortable. Even harder were the emotional burdens placed on a mother when the head of the household, the father, was not there to make the important decisions. The anxiety created by separation and fear of their unknown futures was overwhelming.

East Lillooet camp

Akira Horii stands outside his East Lillooet shack. He remembers how hard even water and power were to get.

Akira Horii:

"Drinking water, trucked in by the barrel, had to be paid for. In the wintertime, snow was melted for drinking. Water for washing and bathing was pumped from the muddy Fraser River, filtered and stored in holding tanks nearby. We hauled it on our backs in five-gallon cans. There was no electricity. Wood was logged in the nearby mountains, trucked to homes, cut, chopped, and stacked by the shack."

Twelve Years Old in Lemon Creek

On September 2, 1942, twelve-year-old Mary Ohara and her family left the horrors of Hastings Park. They were sent to the unknown wilds of the quickly constructed Lemon Creek internment camp in the BC interior. For the children, the train and bus rides were an adventure. "There was so much to see and we made new friends. I tried to hide my excitement because I could sense that my mother was worried. She had lots to be anxious about."

Sharing a shack

"When we reached Lemon Creek, my mother's anxieties worsened. The 'town' was an abandoned cow pasture; our 'home' was an uninsulated shack measuring only 14 x 24 feet (3.5 x 4 m). We had to share it with another family." Here, Mary (back left), four siblings, and her mother pose outside their badly constructed cabin. Notice the primitive equipment by the door used for washing clothes. There was no running water, so water was trucked in daily and had to be heated on a wood stove.

Chapter 5: Internment and Forced Labour

Outhouses

There was no indoor plumbing in the shacks. Trips to the outhouse became an unpleasant part of daily life, especially in the winter. "The pungent odour of lime for the privies brought back memories of Hastings Park," Mary Ohara recalls.

Cold comfort

Each shack contained one kitchen that was shared between the two families who lived there. Like this cabin from the New Denver camp, its only source of heat was a small wood-burning stove.

Mary Ohara:

> "We (the two families) alternated between having our meals in the kitchen and in the bedroom where we used the beds as dining tables. The first winter was unbelievable. We were always cold. We had to scrape the ice off the walls and ceiling in our cabin before the pot-bellied stove was lit and puddles formed on the floor. But we were better off than the families who were still living in canvas tents because not enough shacks were built."

Twelve Years Old in Lemon Creek   103

Mary Ohara:

"Spring arrived in Lemon Creek and brought warm weather and good news; a school was to open in April. The elders and mothers had begged and petitioned the BC Security Commission for a school but it was the last to be completed since there was no electricity. At last the double desk and double chairs, made by elderly issei carpenters were brought into the two-storey building. The 500 elementary students were taught by nisei teachers. It almost felt 'normal.' Although I lost more than a year of schooling, I successfully completed grade eight thanks to the dedicated teachers. I worked hard, too, and looked forward to attending high school in the fall."

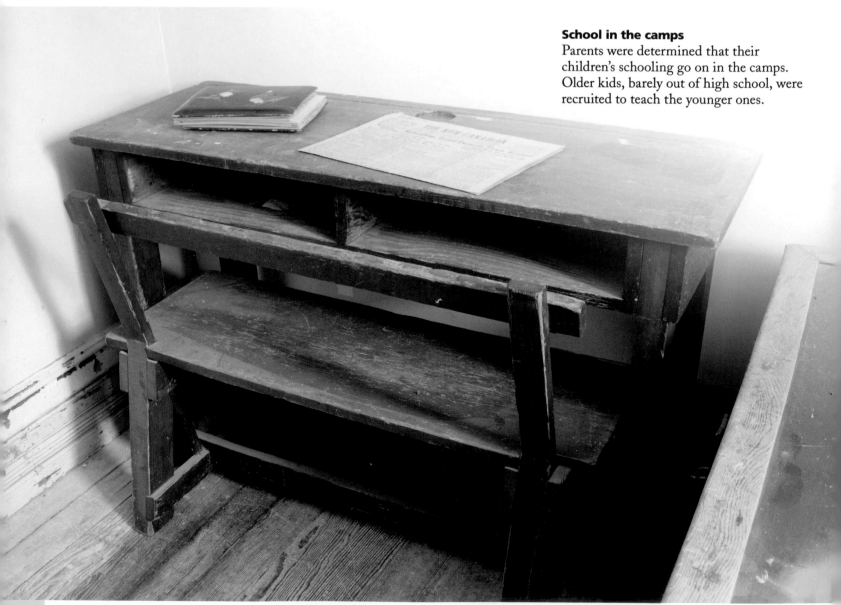

School in the camps
Parents were determined that their children's schooling go on in the camps. Older kids, barely out of high school, were recruited to teach the younger ones.

High school at last
Like the students in this photo from Slocan internment camp, the seventy-five or so high-school students at Lemon Creek attended classes organized by the Catholic Church. Some students continued to take correspondence courses for subjects not offered by the small school.

Mary Ohara:

"We made snowmen, had snowball fights, and played hockey on the frozen creek. With equipment fashioned from leftover lumber, we went skiing, sledding, and tobogganing on the surrounding hills. For a time, the majestic natural surroundings let us forget the grim reality of living in an internment camp."

Making their own fun
Although internment camp was a hardship they should never have been forced to endure, kids were still able to play and have fun at times. Here, a group of Brownies is shown under their handmade sign.

A High-School Student in Greenwood

GREENWOOD

Father Benedict, who had been ministering to the Japanese Canadians in Steveston, saw the potential of the small town of Greenwood, BC. He persuaded Mayor Ted William McArthur that the Japanese Canadians would help revive the local economy. From the Canadian government's perspective, Greenwood was an ideal location for an internment camp. It was isolated from major transportation routes and surrounded by rugged terrain. The once-thriving silver mining town of 6,000 had become a ghost town with a population of about 200. Any opposition from the locals could be dealt with easily. There were empty buildings, dilapidated but still standing, that could be divided into rooms. So, Greenwood became the first internment camp and was designated as a Catholic town, although there were also United Church families and ministers there. The first group of internees arrived on April 25, 1942. Mary Haraga and her family arrived shortly after.

Mary Haraga:
"The buildings were in various stages of disrepair. We were given two rooms (for my mother and eleven children) with beds stacked against the wall with barely enough space for our family to sleep. I hated the lack of privacy."

Crowded living
The crowded conditions of the small cabins is evident in this photo.

Night duty

Like the New Denver camp pictured here, Greenwood had outhouses. Mary recalls, "At night, my younger siblings woke me to accompany them with a flashlight. They were certain that ghosts lived in the latrine!"

June 1945   The Commercial Class
Teacher: Sr. Mario Arduin S.A.
National Film Board of Canada

Typing class for girls

A group of teenaged girls learn to type in class at Greenwood. Mary Haraga wasn't so lucky.

Mary Haraga:

"For a time, Japanese Canadians were not allowed to attend the local school but by the time I was ready for high school, we were accepted. I was so happy to be in high school but it didn't last long. I had to quit after only a few months and find work to help my family out financially."

Mary Haraga:

"The first winter was especially harsh. The house had no insulation and we scratched the frost off the walls. The icy water in the metal tub made me cry out in pain whenever I did the laundry. I wished we had the washing machine we had to leave behind in Abbotsford."

Icy cold

A wood stove was the Haragas' only source of heat.

A High-School Student in Greenwood   107

New Denver

New Denver was a ghost town in the BC interior that had shrunk to a population of 300 people by 1942. There were five camps situated in the area, including one known as "The Orchard" that was located on Slocan Lake. About 1,500 Japanese Canadians were sent to New Denver during the war, some to reside in the sanatorium that was built to care for patients with tuberculosis. Today, New Denver is home to the only sizeable post-war Japanese-Canadian population in BC.

Internment camp shacks
The internees were housed in small wooden cabins built in rows. Each building was shared by two families. These shacks are some of the original buildings preserved at the Nikkei Internment Memorial Centre in New Denver.

"About 1,500 Japanese Canadians were sent to New Denver."

Cooking over a fire

Internees brought essentials with them, including cooking pots like the ones shown here. Cooking was done on wood stoves, which also served to heat the cabins. The stoves could not fully heat the drafty rooms and residents suffered during the cold winters.

Two families in each cabin

Each cabin was divided into three areas: a central kitchen with a sleeping area for one of the two families on each side. The families shared the kitchen and took turns cooking, cleaning, and eating there.

Road Camp and Prison Camp

In March 1942, the British Columbia Security Commission in charge of the internment decided that all male Japanese Canadians eighteen or older would be sent to road camp. They were separated from their families and sent off to remote locations to perform forced labour. Although the living conditions were bad, and the pay of twenty-two to twenty-five cents an hour well below subsistence level, it was the worry about their families that led some men to fight for their rights, even if it meant going to prison camp in Ontario.

Forced separation

There were many tears as men were forced to leave their wives and children and sent off to road camp. Sometimes it was weeks or months before the families found out where their husbands or teenaged sons were located and how they were doing.

Resistance meant prisoner-of-war camp

All male Japanese nationals aged eighteen to forty-five, or military age, were required to go to work in road camps. The men shown here were headed for Jasper, Alberta. Nisei of the same age were to be sent nearly 2,000 miles (3,200 km) away to a road camp in Schreiber, Ontario. When word of the plan became known, some men due to leave from Hastings Park protested and refused to go. In the end, about two-thirds of the original group ended up in Schreiber, some were sent to a work camp near Revelstoke, BC, and several hundred others were sent to a prisoner-of-war camp in northern Ontario as punishment for their defiance.

"You'll be sent east"

June Fujiyama's brother, Taro, left their home to visit a friend several days after Pearl Harbor, and the family did not hear from him again for more than six months. He had been detained by the police and his car had been impounded. Being a Japanese national, born in Japan, he was in the first group of men who were sent to the Yellowhead–Blue River Highway Road Camp Project based in Decoigne, Alberta, pictured here in 1942. Taro spent his first winter in a railroad car until bunks were built.

June Fujiyama:

"Although the conditions in the road camps were deplorable, if there was any protest about the living arrangements or the dangerous working conditions, such as a drunken powder man, the threat was 'you'll be sent east.' For most men it was enough to keep them quiet since being sent to Ontario meant leaving their families behind in BC."

Ghost-town girls

By the end of summer 1942, the BCSC had changed its mind about the road camp policy and most married men were allowed to join their families in the internment camps. But Taro was single, like many of the young men in this photo, and had to remain in road camp. June relates his story: "The 'boys' were in their late teens or their twenties. They counted the days for the once-a-month day pass to a nearby town. They usually went to a movie or restaurant or bought a magazine or ice-cream cone, but what they wanted most was to see girls! They wanted to visit ghost towns where the 'ghost-town girls' outnumbered the boys and competition was slim. When Taro was finally allowed to leave the road camp, he joined our family in Greenwood. There he met his future wife."

Prisoner-of-war camp

By the end of 1942, 699 Japanese-Canadian men were incarcerated in this POW camp in Angler, Ontario. Some of these men were there because they had protested separation from their families. Others were accused of being Japanese military sympathizers who could not be trusted outside the barbed-wire fence. Harry Yonekura was a volunteer with the Steveston's Fishermen's Association, helping the wives and children of Japanese Canadians who had been shipped off to road camp. Japanese nationals were the first to go. When all Japanese-Canadian men were sent away, the RCMP gave extension papers to some volunteers to stay and help with the relocation of the families left behind. When Harry witnessed a mother with two children on her knees begging an RCMP officer to let her go to road camp with her husband, Harry stopped volunteering, tore up his extension paper, and became an activist. He was sent to Angler for his defiance. In prison camp, Harry noted that many of his fellow inmates had been imprisoned for minor things, such as missing curfew. None of the prisoners were ever found guilty of disloyalty to Canada.

"In protest, they went on strike. As punishment, they were sent to the POW camp."

Internee, prisoner, and author

Takeo Nakano, pictured here in the 1980s, was a prisoner at Angler POW camp. He and several others had been at a road camp in the interior of BC and were promised they would be reunited with their families once the work was done. Instead, the BCSC sent them to another road camp. In protest, they went on strike. As punishment, they were sent to the POW camp. Mr. Takano wrote a book about his experiences at road camp and in Angler entitled *Within the Barbed Wire Fence*.

Road Camp and Prison Camp

Camp Baseball

In pre-war Vancouver, the all-Japanese-Canadian Asahi baseball team were the pride of the Powell Street community. During internment, all the team members were dispersed to different camps. In East Lillooet, a self-supporting camp, one young team member created a baseball team among the sagebrush and tumbleweeds to rekindle pride and raise community spirits. Akira Horii was interned in East Lillooet and tells of how baseball ended up bringing the Japanese-Canadian and local white communities closer.

Not welcome
Akira, pictured here, was not quite eleven years old when his family left for the camp.

Akira Horii
"When I awoke from a restless night on the train we had reached the town of Lillooet. It was once a booming gold town, but was now a ghost town. The Japanese were not welcome here. We were to be relocated 10 km east and across the Fraser River in East Lillooet. A bridge separated the two communities."

Akira Horii:
"To enter Lillooet from our internment camp, a special permit was required from the RCMP. We crossed the bridge to see a movie or to shop for groceries. The locals soon realized that the internees did not cause any trouble and that we were good for local businesses, but the barriers stayed up. What started the change in relations was baseball."

Akira Horii:

"Among the internees was Kaye Kaminishi, pictured here, a member of the famous Asahi baseball team who was a sixteen-year-old rookie in the 1939–1940 baseball season. In Japantown before the war, businesses closed their doors to watch the Asahis play at home in Oppenheimer Park. Their games were followed fanatically by both Japanese and non-Japanese fans. Kaye's teammates were now scattered across Canada, but internees needed something to cheer about. Why not form a team here in East Lillooet?"

Akira Horii:

"With help from his fellow internees, Kaye Kaminishi marked out the diamond in the field of sagebrush. They filled rice sacks with dirt for the bases. When the pitcher's mound was built, the field was ready. Suddenly, bats, balls, and a glove or two appeared from old suitcases and rucksacks. Soon grown-ups and children once again heard 'play ball' as they gathered under the hot Lillooet sun. Kaye taught the other players all his skills and proudly wore the Asahi jersey, which he took with him to East Lillooet. Finally his team was ready to challenge the local teams. With help from a police officer, the nisei team was allowed to go into town to play against the locals. No one can remember who won the first tournament, but it was the beginning of something better. Barriers started coming down and the bridge that once separated the locals from us became one that united our two communities."

Forced Labour on the Prairies

Mickey Nakashima was fourteen years old when her father opted to keep his family together. He decided to head to the prairies to work in the fields instead of going to an internment camp. "We were familiar with farm work, were promised fair wages, free housing, public school education, welfare, and medical services. We were unaware, however, that the major cities and smaller towns were out of bounds to the Japanese and that we were to be shipped out of Alberta when the war was over." Some of the Albertan farmers believed the propaganda in the BC press and were worried that they were importing dangerous enemy aliens into their midst, but they desperately needed labourers. Families that ended up in Manitoba found conditions were much better than in Alberta and the people more hospitable and tolerant. By the end of 1942, nearly 4,000 Japanese Canadians were working as labourers on prairie sugar-beet and other farms.

"It was like a slave traders' market"
Mickey's family arrived in Alberta on a guarded train. Families piled onto the backs of trucks, trailers, or horse-drawn wagons, like the one pictured here in 1943 with a group of beet harvesters in southern Alberta.

Mickey Nakashima:

"At long last the truck came to a stop in front of a little shack surrounded by a field. The shack had been built for migrant workers who spent only a few weeks in it during harvest time and was not meant for winter occupancy. It had one layer of siding and a small stove. The rooms were sparsely furnished with a table, a few chairs, and beds. We added the bare essentials we were allowed to bring. Water had to be carted from the irrigation ditch in buckets, which my father tied to both ends of a pole and slung over our shoulders. It was then stored in large barrels, sprinkled with alum, and left for the mud to settle in the bottom before it was ready for drinking. We had to abandon the daily baths which were a ritual for Japanese families."

Mickey Nakashima:

"We put on our 'Sunday best' and stepped off the coach. We stood straight and tall and tried to look older and bigger so that the farmers would see that we were big enough to work. They looked us over. When I think about it, it was like a slave traders' market. As each farmer found his family, he pointed his index finger, said 'you and you,' and nodded his head to hurry and follow him."

Forced Labour on the Prairies

Mickey Nakashima:

"During the week, the responsibility of the beet farm fell on my mother, myself, and my two younger siblings, nine and six. It was backbreaking 'slave' labour."

Slave labour
Mickey's family lived on a corn farm, but there was not enough work to sustain them through the year. Her father negotiated a contract with a local sugar-beet farm, like the one pictured here in Raymond, Alberta, and also found himself work as a janitor for the Broders Cannery.

The old and the young
The elderly also had to work out in the fields. International Red Cross agents, such as the one shown here in Raymond, visited beet farms to check on conditions. Some beet workers got together and complained about farmers who treated them badly. They refused to continue working under their contracts until the growers improved working conditions. Some families were able to change farms as a result of their protest.

Mickey Nakashima:

"Weeding and thinning [the beets] in the hot prairie sun was hard, but the hardest was the beet topping in the fall with knives that were too large for our small hands. My mother wrapped rags around the little wrists of my younger siblings to help lift the heavy beets and knock off clumps of soil before the heads were topped and tossed onto the trucks."

Forced Labour on the Prairies

Speaking Out Against Internment

While Japanese Canadians were interned and their homes, businesses, and possessions were sold off without permission, little protest was made by Canadians outside of British Columbia. But in BC there were some who spoke out against the property sell-off and who objected to the treatment of the Japanese-Canadian minority during and after the war. Church groups, civil liberties groups, the Cooperative Commonwealth Federation (CCF) party (the forerunner of today's New Democratic Party), and others disagreed with the suspension of civil rights to these people. The Japanese Canadians themselves organized and took their fight to court — but without any success.

Justice denied

On March 31, 1943, a group of internees at Kaslo formed the Japanese Property Owners' Association to take legal action to stop the confiscation and sell-off of their properties. In less than a week, the other camps had created similar groups and they joined together in their legal battle. They were devastated when the Canadian justice system failed them by dismissing their case on a technicality. This photo shows the Langham Hotel, where many Japanese Canadians were interned in Kaslo, BC. It is now restored as a museum and art gallery.

King George reviews Japanese-American Soldiers in Italy.
—Courtesy of "New Canadian"

by
HOWARD NORMAN AND THE CONSULTATIVE COUNCIL
(ALL RIGHTS RESERVED **10c**

Ashamed of the past

BC resident Harry Briere bought one of the confiscated Japanese-Canadian fishing boats in the 1940s. When his daughter Elaine, pictured here with a photo of the boat, learned how her father had acquired the boat, she asked him questions. She was shocked and disappointed when he responded with racist comments about the Japanese. "It just goes to show you people who are good citizens in their own community can be irresponsible toward other races. Since then, I've felt ashamed my own father would do that." Elaine felt strongly that wartime injustices should be acknowledged by the government and that the Japanese Canadians should be compensated for their losses and suffering. "It is important that ethics and fairness become a part of Canadian life. Not just saying it, but doing it."

"What about the Japanese Canadians?" (Opposite page)

Reverand Howard Norman was president of the Vancouver Consultative Council for Cooperation in Wartime Problems of Canadian Citizenship. He regarded the proposed sell-off of all Japanese possessions as a similar policy to the Nazis who dispossessed the Jews in Germany. His 1945 pamphlet, "What about the Japanese Canadians?," pictured here, outlined his views about the unfair treatment of the minority.

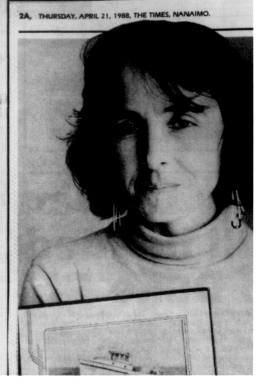

A long-ago wrong is still a wrong

2A, THURSDAY, APRIL 21, 1988, THE TIMES, NANAIMO.

Elaine Briere has a personal reason for supporting the Japanese-Canadian claims for redress for their evacuation from the coast and confiscation of their property.

Her father, Harry Briere, acquired one of the confiscated fishing boats in the early 1940s. He renamed the 30-foot gillnetter, calling it *Poromer*, and fished it out of Prince Rupert.

"He got it for next to nothing," she says. He fished it successfully, and eventually moved into larger boats.

"He became quite well-to-do, but the funny part was all the material things didn't make a happy home-life," she says.

"He was never a happy person, and I think it had a lot to do with this boat."

Briere, a Ladysmith photojournalist, supports the redress movement launched by the National Association of Japanese-Canadians. And she wants to apologize for the injustice.

As a young adult, she learned the origin of the *Poromer* and asked her father for details. "He wouldn't give us any," she says. "Instead he made derogatory comments about the Japanese."

But she says racist attitudes were common during those times. "It was quite typical. It just goes to show you people who are good citizens in their own community can be irresponsible toward other races.

"Since then, I've felt ashamed — ashamed my own father would do that."

She feels strongly that the injustices of the war years must be acknowledged and redressed.

Some politicians spoke out

The CCF party opposed the human rights abuses of the Japanese-Canadian minority. Angus MacInnis, MP for Vancouver East, was one of the few BC politicians who spoke out in support of the Japanese Canadians. His wife Grace successfully campaigned among the churches to create schools in the internment camps when both provincial and federal governments had refused to do so. Mr. MacInnis is pictured here in 1930, front row, third from the right.

Japanese Canadians Join the War

When war broke out in 1939, British Columbia refused to allow nisei (children of Japanese immigrants) to enlist, even though Japanese-Canadian volunteers in other parts of Canada were signed up and sent to serve in Europe. Then, in 1941, the federal government announced that all Canadians of "Oriental origin" would be exempt — in fact barred — from military service. The refusal to allow Japanese Canadians to enlist continued until 1945.

On May 6, 1945, the war in Europe was declared over. All attention turned to the war with Japan. Then the allies needed nisei soldiers who could speak Japanese. Although the Americans and Australians were happy to enlist nisei, the Canadian government refused. The British military, however, wanted to recruit Japanese Canadians fluent in Japanese for military intelligence work in Asia. They recruited nisei in Toronto, Hamilton, and London, Ontario, and the internment camps in BC. Ottawa relented in 1945. Many served overseas. They were considered volunteers, officially in the Canadian Intelligence Corps, but actually working for the British in Asia.

The last Japanese-Canadian recruit returned to Canada two years after Japan's surrender. Unlike other returning veterans, nisei who served Canada were not treated with respect. Instead, they were still forbidden from voting or living on the west coast of BC. Toyo Takata, editor of the *New Canadian*, wrote, "Despite the demanding nature of their assignments, none received a commission, whereas a Caucasian performing similar duties would have been promoted from the ranks."

Allowed to join the British army
These nisei volunteers are being sworn in in 1945. Following their training in Brantford, Ontario, they shipped out to Southeast Asia, where their knowledge of the Japanese language was considered a "secret weapon" by the allies.

In training

In 1945, the British recruited Japanese-Canadian servicemen and gave them basic training in Brantford, Ontario, pictured here.

Roy Ito signed up

In January 1945, British army intelligence officers knocked at the door of Roy Ito, a Japanese-Canadian internee, and recruited him. He remembers thinking, "Perhaps the nisei, in fighting with the British army, can accomplish much to add to the final accomplishment when all men will be equal in every sense of the word. We have everything to gain. I signed up." Ito served as a sergeant with the Canadian Intelligence Corps in India and Southeast Asia. This photo of Japanese language students in Vancouver is part of the Roy Ito Collection from the Japanese Canadian National Museum. Part of his wartime diary is available to read online at jcnm.ca.

Teaching Kanji

Kenjiro (Okada) Ballard, pictured here at the blackboard, taught kanji (Japanese characters) to nisei recruits at the S20 base in Ambleside, Vancouver, in 1945. One hundred and sixteen trained linguists served with the Canadian Intelligence Corps in Southeast Asia and were used to question Japanese prisoners, check for potential war criminals, and examine documents.

War Crimes unit

This group of young Japanese-Canadian officers was working with the War Crimes unit in Bangkok in 1945.

Japanese Canadians Join the War

CHAPTER 6
AFTERMATH

Voluntary Deportation

The Canadian government offered Japanese Canadians, including those born in Canada with Canadian citizenship, what was termed "voluntary repatriation" to Japan. The term was misleading: many Japanese Canadians had never been to Japan, and many spoke little or no Japanese. It was deportation, not repatriation.

In early 1945, when the end of the war seemed close, discussions began about what to do with the internees. Many politicians, including Conservative MP from BC Howard Green, campaigned for the deportation of all people of Japanese descent from Canada. Mary Ohara recalls the feeling of dread when they heard the government's decision: "In the spring of 1945 we got word that everyone over sixteen years of age must choose between exile to Japan or resettlement east of the Rockies. If we refused to leave BC, it would be seen as evidence of disloyalty. It was frightening to have an RCMP officer come to the door and ask 'Have you made up your mind? Are you going to Japan?' If we answered 'yes,' the government would pay the transportation and we would be allowed to stay in BC until our departure. If we said 'no,' our income would be cut off and we'd have to leave BC anyway." Those who agreed to be deported were in for a terrible shock.

DEPARTMENT OF LABOUR
CANADA

NOTICE

TO ALL PERSONS
OF JAPANESE RACIAL ORIGIN
HAVING REFERENCE TO MAKING
APPLICATION FOR
VOLUNTARY REPATRIATION TO JAPAN

The Minister of Labour has been authorized by the Government of Canada to make known the following decisions made with respect to persons of Japanese ancestry, now resident in Canada, who make voluntary application to go to Japan after the war, or sooner where this can be arranged:

1. The net proceeds realized from the disposition of their property, real and personal, in Canada, and standing to their credit at time of repatriation, will be secured to them and may be transferred by them to Japan upon repatriation following the close of the war.

2. In the case of persons sent to Japan under any agreement for exchange of Nationals between Canada and Japan before the close of war, under which agreement the amount of personal property and funds carried by the repatriates is limited, the Custodian of Enemy Alien Property will be authorized, on the advice of the Department of External Affairs, to provide such Japanese repatriates with receipts showing the property left behind in Canada, or net proceeds of same if sold, with a view to their being permitted to secure possession of their property or the net proceeds thereof after the end of hostilities.

3. Free passage will be guaranteed by the Canadian Government to all repatriates being sent to Japan, and all their dependents who accompany them, and including free transportation of such of their personal property as they may take with them.

The above assurances will apply to such persons as have already made written application in satisfactory form to the Government of Canada to go to Japan, or who make written application hereafter for that purpose to the Government of Canada within the period of time fixed by the Commissioner of Japanese Placement for the completion and filing of applications.

These assurances do not apply to persons of the Japanese race repatriated on other than a voluntary basis.

Dated at Ottawa this 13th day of February, 1945.
HUMPHREY MITCHELL
Minister of Labour.

Go "back" to Japan

The Canadian government posted this offer of "repatriation" in February 1945. It was clear that if Japanese Canadians didn't volunteer to go to Japan, they would be sent somewhere else. Going back to their BC homes was never an option. Their homes had been sold or destroyed. Also, despite the fact that the war was over, Japanese Canadians were still not allowed to live on the coast in BC. Japanese Canadians who tried to return to the coast were arrested and put in jail.

The A bomb drops on Nagasaki
The end of the war with Japan finally came when the Allies dropped the second atomic bomb, pictured here in Nagasaki (the first was on Hiroshima). The devastation and loss of lives was enormous. The Japanese government, faced with more atomic bombs and an imminent invasion, surrendered.

"Everyone over sixteen years of age had to choose between exile to Japan or resettlement east of the Rockies."

Forced to leave, again
These small children clutch their few belongings as they wait to leave internment in BC and head to Japan, a land unknown to them.

Voluntary Deportation

A different Japan

The Japan that Mary's mother had left more than twenty-five years previously was very different from the one she was going back to. The Japanese had suffered terribly during the war from bombing raids, such as the one pictured here in Tokyo in 1944. There was desperate poverty due to the massive expense of the war effort. Japan, too, had lost thousands of young men in the war and was in dire condition.

"We had no choice"

Like these children pictured in Slocan in 1946, Mary Ohara and her siblings had to leave Canada when their mother agreed to be sent back to Japan. "My mother wanted to see her own mother, who was living in a remote village in Japan. She had not returned to visit her birthplace since she came as a picture bride in the 1920s. Furthermore, she was a penniless widow with five teenage children, one of whom was mentally challenged. She found the prospect of going east, to yet another unknown and hostile place, too frightening. We had no choice in the matter. We had to abide by our mother's decision."

Mary Ohara:

"I was so sad to leave my friends behind and also anxious about what may lie ahead. The crossing of the Pacific was uneventful but when we docked in Uraga, Japan, we witnessed an incident which was like a forewarning of things to come. As the longshoremen started pulling on the ropes to secure the ship, a couple of sailors from the ship came on deck and threw pieces of bread onto the shore. The longshoremen dropped the lines and scrambled for the crumbs in competition with each other and the seagulls. I laughed, thinking it was some sort of a game. My laughter turned to tears when I was served my first meal on shore. It was a bucket of mixed gruel that smelled like pig food. How I wished for the bread crumbs."

Shipping out
Seventeen-year-old Mary Ohara and her family boarded the *General M.C. Meigs*, pictured here in June 1946.

Voluntary Deportation

Mary Ohara:

"Nothing had prepared us for the devastation in the aftermath of the atom bombs dropped on Hiroshima [seen here] and Nagasaki. We were confronted by scene after scene of bombed-out homes, crudely made shacks, charred remains of indistinguishable objects, people in rags huddled for shelter and children walking aimlessly or digging in the rubble. I thought to myself, 'Mother has made a big, big mistake.' I tried very hard to fit in, but I found that I couldn't. I was a gaijin (a foreigner) in Japan and a Canadian at heart."

Japan after the war
The devastation caused by the atomic bomb in Hiroshima.

"I was a gaijin (a foreigner) in Japan and a Canadian at heart."

Deportation finally stopped
Nearly 4,000 Japanese Canadians were sent to Japan before the Canadian government acknowledged the protests of churches, media, civil-rights activists, and some politicians and stopped the deportations. This photo of Japanese Canadians being repatriated from Slocan hangs in the Nikkei Internment Memorial Centre in New Denver.

Relocation East of the Rockies

Some families opted to leave for eastern Canada following Pearl Harbor, instead of facing internment. Those who stayed in BC during the war and chose not to go to Japan were strongly encouraged to relocate east of the Rockies once the war was over. Going back to the BC coast was not an option they had. Some internees that had gone to the prairies chose to stay there. Others left for further east, to Ontario, Quebec, and the Maritimes. About 13,000 Japanese Canadians decided to go east.

Avoiding internment

When the war came, the Kishimoto family from Cumberland, BC, decided to leave their dairy farm, pictured here, and move to Ontario, instead of facing internment and separation. In St. Thomas, Ontario, they began a successful vegetable farm, mainly supplying a large potato-chip factory.

"About 13,000 Japanese Canadians decided to go east."

New home, new job
Tadachi Nakama went east to make a new life in Ontario. He got a job with Acme Trucking in Geraldton, Ontario, and is pictured here in front of his truck in 1950.

A fresh start
Mr. and Mrs. Aihoshi Baba left BC for Chatham, Ontario. They are pictured here in 1950 in front of Baba's truck, which advertises his new electrical business.

A difficult decision
Mickey Nakashima's family was working in the beet fields of Alberta when the government's "go east" policy was announced. Mickey's family moved to Montreal, where this photo was taken, to join her brother in December 1944. She was the only Japanese Canadian at her high school.

Mickey Nakashima:

"My parents chose to go east. BC held too many painful memories. Remaining in Alberta did not hold much of a future either. There were too many restrictions. It was a difficult decision for my parents, especially since it meant putting more distance between us and my elder sister, who was stranded in Japan. It was also frightening. The newspapers carried terrible anti-Japanese sentiments. Montreal was not a closed city like Toronto was, but similar negative opinions were being reported."

Gratitude from Greenwood

The town of Greenwood had welcomed the internees in 1942. When the war was over, it asked them to stay on, despite the provincial government's push to move all Japanese Canadians out of BC. Mary Haraga's family accepted the invitation and stayed until 1951 before returning to the coast. The plaque pictured here was put up in Greenwood in 1992, celebrating fifty years since the Japanese arrived in Greenwood. Some families stayed on in the community after the coastal restrictions were lifted, making Greenwood their permanent home.

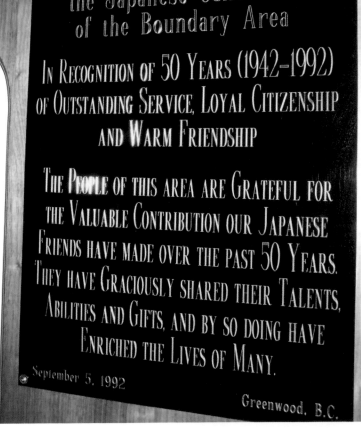

Presented to
the Japanese Canadians
of the Boundary Area

In Recognition of 50 Years (1942–1992)
of Outstanding Service, Loyal Citizenship
and Warm Friendship

The People of this area are Grateful for
the Valuable Contribution our Japanese
Friends have made over the past 50 Years.
They have Graciously shared their Talents,
Abilities and Gifts, and by so doing have
Enriched the Lives of Many.

September 5, 1992

Greenwood, B.C.

Return to the Coast

When the *War Measures Act* was lifted in December 1945, there was hope in the Japanese-Canadian community that they could return to their old neighbourhoods on the BC coast and perhaps begin again. In the United States, Japanese Americans had already returned to the west coast, even before the end of the war. But the hopes of Japanese Canadians were dashed. The government extended the restrictions against Japanese Canadians, banning them from returning to the coast until April 1, 1949. The war was over, but Japanese Canadians were still being treated like enemies. When the ban was finally lifted, only a fraction of the pre-war numbers of Japanese Canadians returned to the coast to start again. In 1941, BC was home to 95.5 per cent of Canada's Japanese-Canadian population. In 1947, following the government's "leave BC" campaign, the Japanese-Canadian population in BC had dropped to 33 per cent of the Canadian total. Some Japanese Canadians did not return to the coast, but settled in the interior of BC instead.

Returning to the fisheries
Many former fishermen could not return to their trade as they had no boats or equipment to come back to. But when some Japanese-Canadian fishermen did come back to the coast, they were not always welcomed. As Mickey Nakashima recounts, "There were stories of fishermen in Steveston who had their nets cut and their boats vandalized." After a great deal of struggle and negotiation, the Japanese-Canadian, Aboriginal, and white fishermen managed to unite under one union and share the resources. A few Japanese Canadians continue to fish off the coast in the twenty-first century. Here, a group of them gather for a potluck on a west coast dock.

Doctor Horii
In 1949, Akira Horii was ready to get on with his life. He entered the University of British Columbia in Vancouver and finished his first year before being pressured into joining his father in the family fishing business. After three years, Akira went back to complete his undergraduate degree before going to medical school. He graduated as a doctor in 1960, becoming one of four Japanese-speaking physicians in Vancouver. He's pictured here in 1995 with one of the many babies he delivered in his long career.

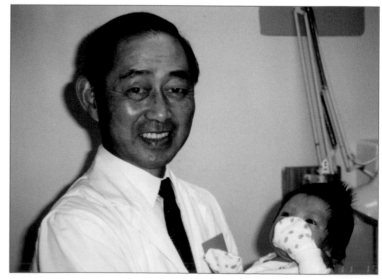

Back to Vancouver

In 1951, Mary Haraga's parents left Greenwood for Vancouver with her youngest siblings, leaving Mary and the older children behind. "With the meagre savings my parents had accumulated, they started all over again. They bought a dry-cleaning store and lived in the back. Soon afterwards, they sent for the rest of us. I left Greenwood the same way I arrived; only with what I could carry." Mary worked at the Jericho School for the Blind. She then married Ike Okabe in 1955, pictured here at their wedding.

"With the meagre savings my parents had accumulated, they started all over again."

After graduating with a degree in Biochemistry from McGill University in Montreal, Mickey Nakashima became a lab tech at the university. She was asked to join her boss at the University of British Columbia Medical School in Vancouver in 1950. Mickey would have passed by these gates, the old entrance to the University.

Mickey Nakashima:

"I accepted the job at UBC, but only after receiving assurances from the president, Dr. Norman Mackenzie, that there would be no racial prejudice practised at UBC. I left BC in tears in 1942, feeling that my own country had abandoned me. I returned in June 1950 with high hopes for a wonderful future."

Mary Ohara:

"I have told my story many times to my children and grandchildren and to the students who visit the National Nikkei Museum and Heritage Centre [pictured here in Burnaby, BC]. I want the younger generation to learn from my life's experiences and to make positive contributions in their lives. My life is fulfilled ... almost. I still dream that one day I will receive a high-school diploma."

One more wish

When news reached Mary Ohara that Japanese Canadians were once again allowed on the BC coast in 1949, she knew she would return from her exile in Japan. Saving every penny for the next five years, she got the $280 needed for her passage and set sail in June 1954. Initially she worked as a domestic for a local doctor, but soon landed a job with Nippon Yusen Kaisha, the Japan Mail Steamship Line, to help returning Japanese Canadians through customs and with the paperwork.

Post-war Life for Japanese Canadians

Although the war ended in 1945, discrimination against Japanese Canadians continued. They were banned from living on the BC coast until 1949. Along with First Nations peoples, they were not allowed to vote in BC until 1949. That was a year later than Japanese Canadians outside of BC and two years after BC had restored the vote to citizens of Chinese and East Indian descent. Many Japanese Canadians did return to the coast once the ban was lifted, but they could never recover what was lost. Not only were their homes and businesses gone, but their communities had been widely dispersed.

How they dealt with the injustice of their treatment during the war depended a lot on their age. Most issei resigned themselves to the past and started again. Many nisei decided that assimilation into white society might be the road to a better future. "The returning nisei of my generation wanted to believe that the Canadian government embodied the British fair play that we were taught in school and we were not ready to admit that we had been betrayed. We wanted to believe that the government had good reasons for the expulsion, dispossession, and deportation, and preferred to blame ourselves for what happened," explains Mary Haraga. Many second-generation and later Japanese Canadians have gone on to great success in politics, business, professional pursuits, the arts, and sports, with several being inducted into the Order of Canada.

"We wanted to believe that the government had good reasons for the expulsion, dispossession, and deportation."

Property recovered: the only case

Zennosuke Inouye immigrated to Canada in 1900 and served as a soldier for his new country in World War One. Wounded, he returned from the war and purchased land in Surrey, BC, through the government's soldier settlement plan. He cleared the land, planted berries, raised a family — pictured here — and developed a successful farming business. In 1942, he and his family were evacuated. His land was eventually transferred from the Custodian of Enemy Alien Property to the Director of *Veterans' Land Act*. The plan was to sell confiscated Japanese-Canadian properties to returning soldiers of the Second World War. Mr. Inouye protested the sale of his land and wrote many letters to officials before and after the end of the war. Eventually he appealed to his former Commanding Officer and to the Royal Commission on Japanese-Canadian Claims, known as the Bird Commission. In 1949, his land was returned to him. He was the only individual Japanese Canadian to get his property back.

Starting all over again
Mrs. Chiba returned to Vancouver in 1951 and started her dressmaking business, shown here in 1959. Like her, Mary Haraga's parents struggled to build a new family business in Vancouver.

Mary Haraga:

> "Issei like my parents were having to come to terms with the loss of everything that had taken them a lifetime to build and the complete disappearance of the world as they knew it. Their belief in gaman (patience and perseverance) and shikataganai ('it can't be helped') enabled them to endure the pain, sorrow, shame, and mental anguish without breaking."

David Suzuki
More than forty Japanese Canadians have been inducted into the Order of Canada, including Lori Fung, Jon Kimura Parker, Dr. Masajiro Miyazaki, and scientist, author, broadcaster, and environmental activist David Suzuki, pictured here. Mr. Suzuki was a child when he and his family were interned at Slocan during the war.

Joy Kogawa

Order of Canada recipient and author Joy Kogawa is pictured here with her family in the early 1940s in front of a log cabin in Slocan, where they were interned. Ms. Kogawa's award-winning novel *Obasan* tells the story of a young Japanese-Canadian girl sent to an internment camp. Later she continued the story in *Itsuka*, a book that picks up the lives of the original characters when they are older. A book for younger children, *Naomi's Road*, brought the story of internment to a new audience. Joy Kogawa was a driving force in the community's fight for redress.

Remembering the good times

June Fujiyama married during the war and moved with her husband to Midway, BC, a self-supporting community, where he worked in a sawmill. She first worked as a kindergarten teacher and later became a secretary for the school and then for the village office. "Job opportunities that did not exist on the coast were opened to us." In 1970, after their daughters entered university, she and her husband returned to the coast. June now lives in Vancouver. "Over the years I have attended several reunions with people who were relocated. The most recent was in 2008 and held in Toronto where many of the internees had resettled. I enjoy our reunions immensely. My friends and I talk about 'those years' without bitterness. We choose to remember the good times and the bonds we formed that have lasted more than six decades."

Today's Japanese-Canadian communities

Nearly 92 per cent of the Japanese-Canadian population lives in BC, Ontario, or Alberta, with the largest numbers living in Vancouver (pictured here) and Toronto. There are no Japantowns in Canada today. Vancouver organizes the Powell Street Festival in August every year that brings people together for two days to showcase Japanese-Canadian culture. Although Toronto and Montreal have Chinatowns and Little Italies, for example, no Japantowns exist. This is a direct result of the forced dispersal of Japanese Canadians after the end of the war. Because the Japanese-Canadian population was forced to disperse so widely, assimilation became inevitable in many ways. This was, of course, part of the government's agenda — to effectively force assimilation.

A new kind of Japanese-Canadian community

Due to the government's forced dispersal of their parents after the war, third-generation Japanese Canadians, sansei, went to school with mostly non-Japanese Canadians and lived in mostly white neighbourhoods. Therefore it is not surprising that many ended up marrying outside of their culture. According to Statistics Canada, with a 95 per cent rate of marrying outside their ethnic group, Japanese Canadians are considered to be "the most integrated and assimilated group of all the ethnic communities" in Canada. There is now a hapa generation: since hapa means "half" the term has been adopted by Asians to mean "half Asian." Many descendents of the original Japanese immigrants have children and grandchildren with mixed heritage.

Despite the nearly complete destruction of their cultural community, there are many personal success stories that must be attributed to a tradition of placing a high value on education and hard work. Japanese Canadians are nearly twice as likely to have a university degree and have a higher average income than the general population.

Today's Japanese-Canadian community is actually made up of two different groups: those that survived the internment in Canada, and those who immigrated to Canada from Japan after the war. One of the main differences between them is language. Members of the two groups cannot speak to each other since the sansei (third generation) and younger generations cannot converse in Japanese and the issei find it difficult to speak English. Many post-war Japanese immigrants are not aware of how poor Japan was at the turn of the twentieth century. Many openly express surprise that their ancestors left Japan for Canada in search of a better life.

Asian stereotyping

According to the most recent data available from Statistics Canada, almost 40 per cent of the Japanese-Canadian population fifteen years and older reported that they had "experienced either discrimination or unfair treatment based on their ethnicity, race, religion, language or accent in the five years preceding the survey." This recent painting by Roger Shimomura, entitled "Yellow Terror," is described as a "Where's Waldo?" type of collage using pictures from his huge collection of images that portray Asian stereotypes in Western culture. Although racism still exists, there is no more official government racism of the kind that existed in the 1800s and first half of the 1900s in Canada. The *Canadian Charter of Human Rights and Freedoms* guarantees some protection to Canadian citizens and multiculturalism is a valued feature of Canadian society.

Post-war Life for Japanese Canadians

CHAPTER 7
ACKNOWLEDGING THE PAST

Fight for Apology and Redress

In 1977, Japanese-Canadian communities across Canada celebrated the 100th anniversary of the arrival of the first Japanese immigrant, Manzo Nagano. A year of special events not only raised awareness of the contributions of Japanese Canadians to Canadian society, but also raised questions regarding the injustices of the war years. It planted the seeds for a redress campaign headed by the National Association of Japanese Canadians (NAJC). Eleven years of meetings, broken government promises, internal disagreements, rallies, rejected proposals, public pressure, and a government settlement in the United States finally resulted in an agreement between the NAJC and the government of Prime Minister Brian Mulroney. Mickey Nakashima reflects on what it meant to the community: "The acknowledgement, apology, and symbolic compensation to those who were eligible and still living meant that the burden of shame and presumed guilt that issei and nisei had carried for years was lifted. We were finally absolved of any wrongdoing. The greatest regret was for the issei of my parents' generation who had died without witnessing redress."

Protest rally

Seven years into their fight for redress, the NAJC changed tactics. They decided to seek broad-based support for their campaign from other ethnic groups, unions, professional organizations, and religious and cultural groups. There was a huge response. A Toronto protest rally in 1987 was supported by fifteen national ethnic organizations and resulted in the formation of the National Coalition for Japanese Canadian Redress. Famous Canadians such as authors Margaret Atwood, June Callwood, and Pierre Berton supported them. A second rally in April 1988 in Ottawa, shown here, got lots of media attention and was considered a high point in the fight for redress. A national opinion poll at the time showed that a majority of Canadians supported redress. At the same time, there was disagreement amongst the Japanese-Canadian community; some did not support redress for various reasons. Within the movement itself, there was disagreement on what form redress should take — group compensation or individual compensation.

"We were finally absolved of any wrongdoing."

As a people, Canadians commit themselves to the creation of a society that ensures equality and justice for all, regardless of race or ethnic origin.

During and after World War II, Canadians of Japanese ancestry, the majority of whom were citizens, suffered unprecedented actions taken by the Government of Canada against their community.

Despite perceived military necessities at the time, the forced removal and internment of Japanese Canadians during World War II and their deportation and expulsion following the war, was unjust. In retrospect, government policies of disenfranchisement, detention, confiscation and sale of private and community property, expulsion, deportation and restriction of movement, which continued after the war, were influenced by discriminatory attitudes. Japanese Canadians who were interned had their property liquidated and the proceeds of sale were used to pay for their own internment.

The acknowledgement of these injustices serves notice to all Canadians that the excesses of the past are condemned and that the principles of justice and equality in Canada are reaffirmed. Therefore, the Government of Canada, on behalf of all Canadians, does hereby:

1)   acknowledge that the treatment of Japanese Canadians during and after World War II was unjust and violated principles of human rights as they are understood today;

2)   pledge to ensure, to the full extent that its powers allow, that such events will not happen again; and

3)   recognize, with great respect, the fortitude and determination of Japanese Canadians who, despite great stress and hardship, retain their commitment and loyalty to Canada and contribute so richly to the development of the Canadian nation.

Brian Mulroney

Prime Minister of Canada

The Government of Canada's apology

In June 1988, the Canadian government reopened discussions with the redress committee. In August, US President Ronald Regan signed a redress bill with the Japanese-American redress committee, acknowledging the injustices of internment and granting each individual $20,000. It was no coincidence that, only days later, the Canadian government reached an agreement with the NAJC. The government's acknowledgement of wrongdoing is presented here.

Righting Canada's wrong

PM Brian Mulroney and NAJC President Art Miki are seen here signing the redress agreement on September 22, 1988. From left to right in the background are Maryka Omatsu, Roy Miki, Cassandra Kobayashi, Mas Takahashi, Harold Hinrose, and Harry Nishimoto, all members of the Japanese-Canadian community. The main elements of the redress were the official acknowledgement, a symbolic $21,000 per living individual who suffered under the wartime policies, $12 million to be administered by the NAJC for social, cultural, and educational promotion of their community or human rights, and $24 million to establish a Canadian Race Relations Foundation. Some money has been used to fund seniors' facilities and cultural centres where a new sense of pride in Japanese heritage has developed.

Celebrating success

Following the redress-signing ceremony there was a reception. Government officials, supporters of the redress, and Japanese Canadians celebrated together. Pictured on the left is Cassandra Kobayashi, a lawyer who served on the redress committee and who co-authored, with Roy Miki, the book *Justice in Our Time: The Japanese Canadian Redress Settlement*. Bill Kobayashi and Roy Miki are pictured with her.

Fight for Apology and Redress   147

Permanent Acknowledgements

Since the Japanese-Canadian community was dispersed so widely and completely during and after the war, it took a great deal of effort to create new communities across the country, wherever internees ended up. In Vancouver, the Japanese Language School and Hall still exists, and celebrated its 100th anniversary in 2004. The National Association of Japanese Canadians was created in 1947 to help with community development as well as human rights. Over the years, museums and memorials have been dedicated to those who suffered the internment at the hands of the Canadian government. This story needs to be told to new generations so that the tumultuous history of the Japanese in Canada is acknowledged and remembered.

A new light for Stanley Park
This memorial to Japanese-Canadian soldiers from World War One stands in Vancouver's Stanley Park. When Canada declared war on Japan in 1941, the light on the monument was turned out. It was finally relit in 1957.

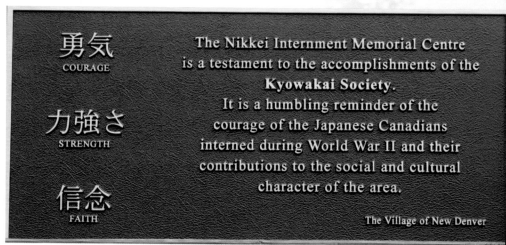

勇気
COURAGE

力強さ
STRENGTH

信念
FAITH

The Nikkei Internment Memorial Centre is a testament to the accomplishments of the **Kyowakai Society.**
It is a humbling reminder of the courage of the Japanese Canadians interned during World War II and their contributions to the social and cultural character of the area.

The Village of New Denver

Nikkei Internment Memorial Centre
This plaque for the Nikkei Internment Memorial Centre in New Denver, BC, welcomes visitors to the site of one of the internment camps. It is the only interpretive centre in Canada dedicated solely to the experiences of Japanese-Canadian internees. Three restored, original shacks are featured at the Centre, along with a number of artifacts and memorabilia that have been collected. Several former internees still live in the community of New Denver and take great pride in the Centre.

Memorial gardens

The Nikkei Internment Memorial Centre in New Denver features these Japanese memorial gardens, dedicated to the internees. Other memorial gardens exist, such as the Momiji Gardens at Hastings Park, the Japanese gardens on Mayne Island and Salt Spring Island, and the Japanese garden in Lethbridge, Alberta.

Greenwood Museum

The first internment centre was in Greenwood, BC. The town's museum, pictured here, has created a display that honours that past and includes many documents and items from the time.

Gulf of Georgia Cannery

The Gulf of Georgia Cannery National Historic Site, pictured here, was established to tell the story of Canada's west coast fishing industry from the 1870s to today. The history of the working cannery and the nearby town of Steveston is entangled with the history of the Japanese immigrants who worked there up until the internment. Some returned to re-establish their fishing rights after the ban was lifted in 1949. In Prince Rupert on the Skeena, the Northern Pacific Cannery is a heritage site that also tells the story of Japanese Canadians in the fishing industry.

The Langham

Kaslo, BC, was a ghost town that became home to an internment centre during the war. The Langham was an old hotel that was converted into accommodation for internee families. It is now a museum where displays, such as this one of an internee's bed and belongings, teach visitors about the internment and the hardships suffered by those who lived there.

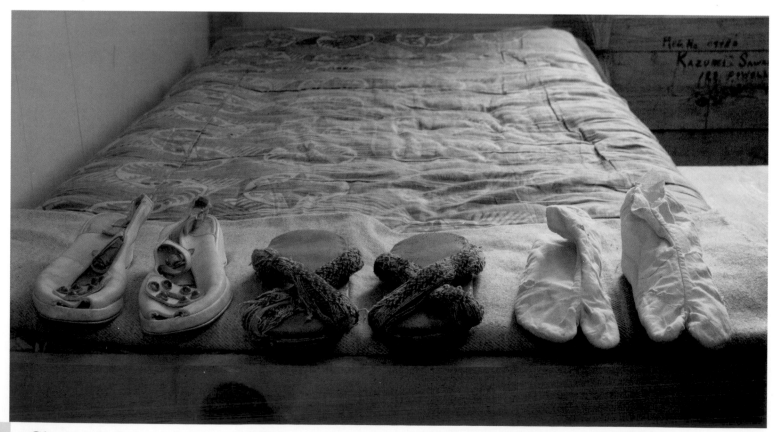

Japanese Canadians in Toronto

The Japanese Canadian Cultural Centre (JCCC) opened in Toronto in 1964. It serves as a gathering point for Japanese Canadians and non-Japanese people alike. It works to introduce the culture, history, and legacy of Japanese Canadians to all. During the opening ceremonies, Prime Minister Lester B. Pearson admitted that the internment during World War Two was a "black mark" in Canadian history. But it was another twenty-four years before the official government apology was given. In 2004, the JCCC opened its new 6,500 square foot Kobayashi Hall in Toronto. It is designed to hold music concerts, festivals, conferences, weddings, and many other large community events.

Shige Yoshida is honoured

In August 1991, the town of Chemainus, BC, unveiled a mural of Shige Yoshida in recognition of his efforts to form the first all-nisei Scout troop in Chemainus. Mr. Yoshida is pictured here with artist Stanley Taniwa of Manitoba.

Permanent Acknowledgements

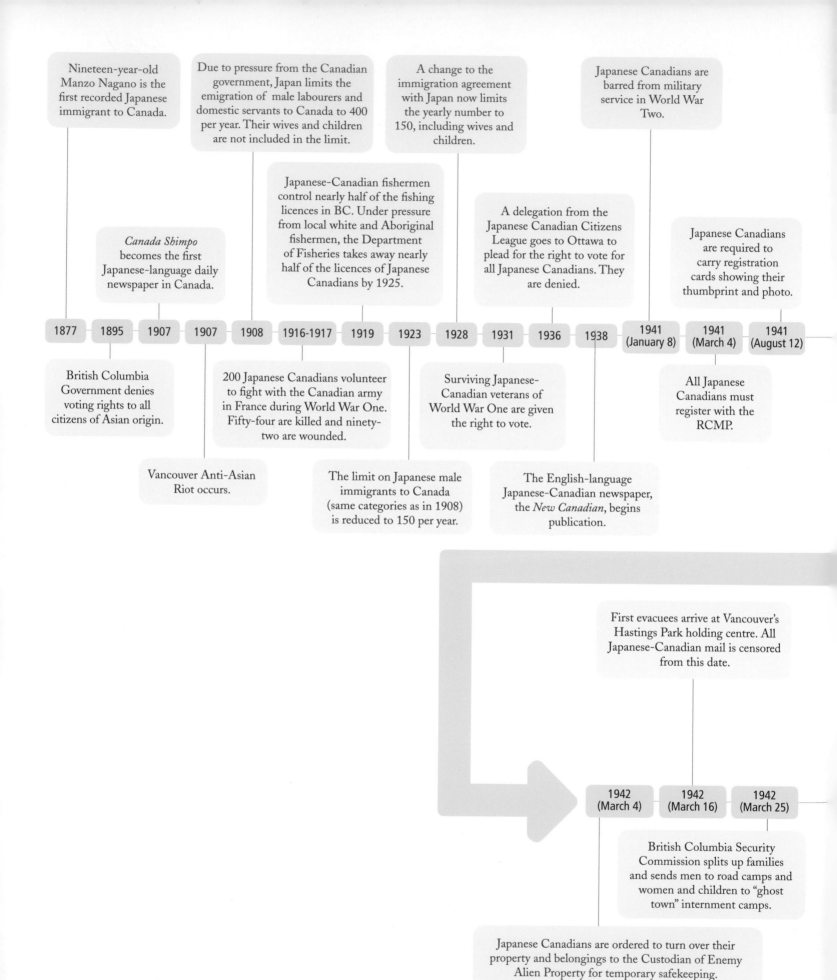

Nineteen-year-old Manzo Nagano is the first recorded Japanese immigrant to Canada.

Due to pressure from the Canadian government, Japan limits the emigration of male labourers and domestic servants to Canada to 400 per year. Their wives and children are not included in the limit.

A change to the immigration agreement with Japan now limits the yearly number to 150, including wives and children.

Japanese Canadians are barred from military service in World War Two.

Canada Shimpo becomes the first Japanese-language daily newspaper in Canada.

Japanese-Canadian fishermen control nearly half of the fishing licences in BC. Under pressure from local white and Aboriginal fishermen, the Department of Fisheries takes away nearly half of the licences of Japanese Canadians by 1925.

A delegation from the Japanese Canadian Citizens League goes to Ottawa to plead for the right to vote for all Japanese Canadians. They are denied.

Japanese Canadians are required to carry registration cards showing their thumbprint and photo.

1877 — 1895 — 1907 — 1907 — 1908 — 1916-1917 — 1919 — 1923 — 1928 — 1931 — 1936 — 1938 — 1941 (January 8) — 1941 (March 4) — 1941 (August 12)

British Columbia Government denies voting rights to all citizens of Asian origin.

200 Japanese Canadians volunteer to fight with the Canadian army in France during World War One. Fifty-four are killed and ninety-two are wounded.

Surviving Japanese-Canadian veterans of World War One are given the right to vote.

All Japanese Canadians must register with the RCMP.

Vancouver Anti-Asian Riot occurs.

The limit on Japanese male immigrants to Canada (same categories as in 1908) is reduced to 150 per year.

The English-language Japanese-Canadian newspaper, the *New Canadian*, begins publication.

First evacuees arrive at Vancouver's Hastings Park holding centre. All Japanese-Canadian mail is censored from this date.

1942 (March 4) — 1942 (March 16) — 1942 (March 25)

British Columbia Security Commission splits up families and sends men to road camps and women and children to "ghost town" internment camps.

Japanese Canadians are ordered to turn over their property and belongings to the Custodian of Enemy Alien Property for temporary safekeeping.

Timeline

1,200 Japanese-Canadian fishing boats are seized by the government. Japanese-language newspapers and schools are shut down.

Mass evacuation of Japanese Canadians begins. Their cars, cameras, binoculars, and radios are seized as "security" measures. A dusk-to-dawn curfew is imposed.

| 1941 (December 7) | 1941 (December 8) | 1942 (February 24) | 1942 (February 26) |

All male Japanese-Canadian citizens between the ages of 18 and 45 are forced to leave the 100-mile-wide restricted zone along the coast of British Columbia. They are sent to road camps.

Japan attacks Pearl Harbour.

Prime Minister Brian Mulroney formally apologizes on behalf of the Canadian Government for the wrongful internment, seizure of property, and the disenfranchisement of thousands of Canadians of Japanese ancestry. A redress settlement is also announced, which includes a symbolic payment to individual survivors.

Japanese Canadians are allowed to join the Allied troops in World War Two and 150 volunteer for service in the Far East.

Federal cabinet cancels its deportation policy after protests by churches, academics, journalists, and some politicians.

Director of Soldier Settlement is given authority to buy or lease confiscated Japanese-Canadian farms. 572 farms are turned over without consulting the owners.

Japan surrenders after atomic bombs are dropped on Hiroshima and Nagasaki.

Japanese Canadians are allowed to return to the coast of BC. They are also given the right to vote in BC.

| 1942 (June 29) | 1943 (January 19) | 1945 (January–May) | 1945 (April 13) | 1945 (September 2) | 1946 (May 31) | 1947 (January 24) | 1948 (June 15) | 1949 (April 1) | 1967 | 1988 (September 22) |

Federal cabinet gives Custodian of Enemy Alien Property the right to sell off Japanese Canadians' property, without owners' consent.

Forced exile to Japan begins. Nearly 4,000 are deported to Japan, many of whom are Canadian citizens

Canadian Government announces a new immigration policy that does not use race as a deciding factor for potential immigrants.

Canadian government begins its "go east" policy, forcing Japanese Canadians living in British Columbia to choose between moving to eastern Canada or being deported to Japan.

Japanese Canadians are given the right to vote in Canada, but not in BC.

Glossary

assimilation: When the culture of a minority or immigrant group becomes lost within the more dominant culture.

bias: A preference or tendency to think or act in a certain way. Bias may be positive or negative.

cannery: A business that cans food for retail sale. Many Japanese immigrants worked in canneries in BC, where fish, such as salmon, caught by local fishermen were put into cans.

censors: People whose job it is to hide or destroy material, often written or broadcast, that is considered politically or morally unacceptable. For example, letters written by Japanese Canadians were opened and read, and in many cases parts were blacked out or cut out. The contents of the only English-language Japanese-Canadian newspaper, the *New Canadian*, had to be approved by a censor before going to press.

citizenship: The country that a person belongs to. When you are a citizen of a country, you can have a passport from the country and receive all the rights and benefits that the country offers.

civil rights: The basic privileges that come with being a member of society in a certain country. Rights such as the right to vote, to have an education, and to receive justice in the courts are civil rights.

compensation: The payment of money to make up for a wrong that was done to a person or group. In the case of Japanese Canadians, the compensation of $21,000 per individual was symbolic. This means that it didn't actually cover the costs of what was lost, but it was an effort to recognize that people did lose a great deal due to the government's actions in the past.

curfew: A police or military rule that required people to keep off the streets after a specific time, often sunset to sunrise.

concentration camp: A term that refers to the crowding together of people in a confined space by authorities. It was used by many nisei during the war to describe the interior settlements, also referred to as internment camps.

delegation: A small group of people who represent a much larger group's ideas or demands.

deportation: The sending away of people from the country where they are living back to the country from whence they came. For example, sending Japanese immigrants living in Canada back to Japan.

discrimination: Unjust actions that are caused by a particular mindset or prejudice. A means of treating people negatively because of their group identity. Discrimination may be based on age, ancestry, gender, language, race, religion, political beliefs, sexual orientation, family status, physical or mental disability, appearance, or economic status. Acts of discrimination hurt, humiliate, and isolate the victim.

dispossession: The taking away of a person's belongings which can include homes, businesses, and personal property.

emigration: Leaving one's home country to move to a different country.

enemy alien: A person of foreign descent living in a country that is at war with his country of ancestry. This was a term used in government notices and in the media to describe all Japanese Canadians as enemies of the state. The term was applied regardless of birthplace or citizenship and required no proof of crimes against Canada.

evacuate: To force a person to move away from a threatened area or place. The term was used for the removal of all people of Japanese ancestry from the "protected area" on the Pacific coastline of British Columbia.

exile: To force a person to leave one's country, community, or province as punishment. At the end of the war, Japanese Canadians were told to move out of British Columbia to another part of Canada or to go to Japan, a country many had never seen.

forced dispersal: A ruling by government or military that requires people to leave their communities and move to other parts of the country or the world.

franchise: The right to vote. Japanese Canadians in British Columbia were denied the franchise — not allowed to vote — in provincial elections until 1948 and in federal elections until 1949. When someone's right to vote is taken away, they are disenfranchised.

gaijin: A Japanese word for foreigner.

gaman: A Japanese term that means patience or perseverance.

ghost town: A community that has lost most of its inhabitants, often because a major employer has moved out and people have had to leave to find work.

hapa: means "half" and comes from *hapa haoli* in Hawaiian. The term has been adopted by Asian Canadians to mean "half Asian."

immigration: The arrival of people into a country from their homeland.

impounded: The seizure of a possession from an individual by the authorities, such as the police or military. Fishing boats, cars, cameras, and other possessions belonging to Japanese Canadians were impounded by the government.

incarceration: Holding someone against their will in a guarded place, such as a jail.

injustice: A wrongful action taken against an individual or group that denies them their basic rights.

in trust: To place something in the care of someone for safekeeping. All property belonging to Japanese Canadians in British Columbia (land, homes, furniture, businesses, cars, etc.) that they were forced to leave behind during the evacuation was given "in trust" to the Custodian of

Enemy Alien Property for safekeeping. This property was later sold without the consent of Japanese Canadians to pay for the internment process. In other words, the government broke their "trust."

internment: The confinement of people labelled enemies of the state during wartime. Thousands of people of Japanese ancestry were forced to leave the west coast of British Columbia and were sent to remote communities in the interior of BC or hastily built camps for the duration of World War Two. Their freedom was severely limited until 1949, four years after the war ended.

internment camp: The place where people who were labelled enemy aliens were sent during the war. There were several different kinds of internment camps for Japanese Canadians.

issei (ees-say): A Japanese-language term to describe the first generation of immigrants

kimono: A traditional Japanese dress-like piece of clothing for women.

nisei (nee-say): A Japanese-language term to describe second generation or Canadian-born children of immigrants

sansei (sun-say): A Japanese-language term to describe the third generation — children born to nisei.

nikkei (neek-kay): A Japanese-language term to describe someone of Japanese descent. "Nikkei Kanadajin" means a Canadian of Japanese descent.

oppression: Occurs when the feelings, ideas, or demands of an individual or group of people are not recognized or allowed to be expressed by authorities such as the government, the justice system, police, or the military.

"picture bride": A term used for the Japanese women who were approached in Japan by families of men who had already moved to Canada. They were shown a picture of the man who was looking for a wife and agreed to come to Canada to marry him.

prejudice: An attitude, usually negative, directed toward a person or group of people based on wrong or distorted information. Prejudiced thinking may result in acts of discrimination.

prison camp: A place where individuals were sent to be guarded by the military during the war. Prisoners-of-war (POWs) were usually citizens of a country that Canada was at war with, or they were individuals who were thought to be a threat to Canada. Some Japanese Canadians were sent to prison camp for refusing to go to road camps, protesting against being separated from their families, breaking curfew, or other minor issues.

propaganda: The spread of specific information, ideas, or images (such as war posters) to influence and control public opinion or actions.

protected area: A place that is designated by authorities to be out-of-bounds for specific people or activities. During World War Two, the government created a 100-mile (about 160 kilometers) wide "secure" zone from the coast of BC to the interior Cascade Mountains. All Japanese Canadians were forced to leave the area "for reasons of security."

racism: A belief that one race is superior to another. People are not treated as equals because of their cultural or ethnic differences. Racism may be systemic (part of institutions, governments, organizations, and programs) or part of the attitudes and behaviour of individuals.

redress: To right a wrong, sometimes by compensating the victim or by punishing the wrongdoer. Redress also refers to the movement within the Japanese-Canadian community for an official apology and payment for the injustices of the government's actions toward Japanese Canadians during World War Two.

registration: A person is required to report to an authority and give his or her name, place of residence, and other personal information, and it is kept on record. All people of Japanese descent who were sixteen years of age or older had to register with the RCMP after Pearl Harbor.

relocation: To move to another place.

repatriation: To send back to one's own country of birth or place of citizenship.

road camp: A category of internment camp where Japanese-Canadian men and boys over eighteen years of age were sent to do forced labour, often work on roads.

sanatorium: A hospital-like facility that cared for people with a disease called tuberculosis.

self-supporting camp: A category of internment camps where men were allowed to stay with their families, but each family had to pay for their own accommodations, schools, teachers, and other basics. Only some Japanese Canadians could afford to go to these camps.

shikataganai: A Japanese term that means "it can't be helped" or "nothing can be done about it."

shinai: A wooden or bamboo stick that is used in the Japanese sport of kendo to replace the traditional swords.

sympathizer: A person who is thought to be in favour of a particular group, policy, or idea. Some people accused Japanese Canadians of being in favour of the Japanese military war efforts, and fought to have them interned even though there was no proof of any disloyalty to Canada.

tenant farmer: Someone who farms land that is owned by someone else and pays rent or crops to the owner.

totalitarian: A type of political system in which one person has absolute control and dictates what everyone else must do. There are no elections for the one in charge. No opposition to the leader is permitted.

tuberculosis: An infection of the lungs that is contagious and may cause death.

visible minority: This is a modern term used to describe people of an ethnic group who have physical features, usually skin colour, that make them distinct from the majority of the population.

War Measures Act: A Canadian law that gave the government the right to label individuals as enemy aliens and take away their civil rights, such as the right to be presumed innocent.

For Further Reading

Intermediate Books/Novels:

Garrigue, Sheila. *The Eternal Spring of Mr. Ito.* New York: Atheneum, 1985.

Kogawa, Joy. *Obasan.* Markham, ON: Penguin Books, 1983.

——. *Itsuka.* Toronto: Viking Canada, 1992.

——. *Naomi's Road.* Toronto: Stoddard Kids, 1986.

Savage, Jeff. *Paul Kariya: Hockey Magician.* Toronto: Monarch Books, 2002.

Takashima, Shizuye. *A Child in Prison Camp.* Toronto: Tundra Books, 1971.

Walters, Eric. *Caged Eagles.* Victoria, BC: Orca Book Publishers, 2000.

Watada, Terry. *Seeing the Invisible: The Story of Irene Uchida.* Toronto: Umbrella Press, 1998.

Yesaki, Mitsuo. *Watari-Dori (Birds of Passage).* Vancouver: Peninsula Publishing, 2004.

Non-fiction Books:

Adachi, Ken. *The Enemy that Never Was.* Toronto: McClelland & Stewart, 1976.

Adachi, Pat. *Asahi: A Legend in Baseball.* Etobicoke: Coronex Printing and Publishing, 1992.

Ashworth, Mary. *The Forces Which Shaped Them: A History of the Education of Minority Group Children in British Columbia.* Vancouver: New Star Books, 1979.

Broadfoot, Barry. *Years of Sorrow, Years of Shame.* Toronto: Doubleday Canada, 1977.

Fukawa, Masako, Stanley Fukawa, and the Nikkei Fishermen History Book Committee. *Spirit of the Nikkei Fleet: BC's Japanese Canadian Fishermen.* Madeira Park, BC: Harbour Publishing, 2009.

Ito, Roy. *We Went to War.* Ottawa: Wings Canada, 1984.

Japanese Canadian Centennial Project. *A Dream of Riches: The Japanese Canadian 1877–1977.* Vancouver, 1978.

Kitagawa, Muriel, and Roy Miki, ed. *This is my Own: Letters to Wes and Other Writings on Japanese Canadians, 1941–1948.* Vancouver: Talonbooks, 1985.

Knight, Rolf. *A Man of Our Times. The Life-history of a Japanese-Canadian Fisherman.* Vancouver: New Star Books, 1976.

Miki, Roy, and Cassandra Kobayashi. *Justice in Our Time: The Japanese Canadian Redress Settlement.* Vancouver: Talonbooks, 1991.

Moritsugu, Frank, and the Ghost Town Teachers' Historical Society. *Teaching in Canadian Exile: A History of the Schools for Japanese Canadian Children in BC Detention Camps during the Second World War.* Toronto: Ghost Town Teachers' Historical Society, 2001.

Nakano, Takeo. *Within the Barbed Wire Fence.* Toronto: University of Toronto Press, 1980.

Nikkei Fishermen's Book Committee. *Nikkei Fishermen on the BC Coast: Their Biographies and Photographs.* Vancouver: Harbour Publishing, 2007.

Oiwa, Keibo, ed. *Stone Voices: Wartime Writings of Japanese Canadian Issei.* Montreal: Véhicule Press, 1991.

Roy, Patricia, J. L. Granatstein, Masako Ino, and Horoko Takamura. *Mutual Hostages: Canadians and Japanese during the Second World War.* Toronto: University of Toronto Press, 1990.

Shibata, Yuko. *The Forgotten History of Japanese Canadians.* Vancouver: New Sun Books, 1977.

Sunahara, Ann. *The Politics of Racism: The Uprooting of Japanese Canadians during the Second World War.* Toronto: Lorimer, 1981

Takata, Toyo. *Nikkei Legacy: The Story of Japanese Canadians from Settlement to Today.* Toronto: New Canada Publications, 1983.

Takashima, Shizue. *A Child in Prison Camp.* Toronto: Tundra Books, 1971

Yesaki, Mitsuo. *Steveston: Cannery Row.* Peninsula Publishing, 1998.

——. *Sutebusuton: A Japanese Village on the British Columbia Coast.* Vancouver: Peninsula Publishing, 2003.

Films:

Mrs. Murakami: Family Album. 1991. Moving Images Distributors. 24 min. www.movingimages.ca. Enters the lives of the Murakami family of Salt Spring Island and gives, first hand, the drama of a chilling history of internment.

Justice in Our Time: How Redress Was Won. 1989. National Association of Japanese Canadians, Jesse Nishihata Productions. 29 min. www.najc.ca. Includes signing of the Redress Agreement between the National Association of Japanese Canadians and the Government of Canada, September 22, 1988.

Enemy Alien. 1975. National Film Board of Canada (NFB). 26 min. www.nfb.ca. Black and white. Tells of Japanese Canadians' long, frustrating struggle for acceptance as Canadians. Viewable online.

Minoru: Memory of Exile. 1992. NFB. 18 min. www.nfb.ca. Colour. A Japanese-Canadian filmmaker tells the story of his Canadian-born father and himself as they were interned and then exiled to Japan. Suitable for younger viewers. Viewable online.

Obachan's Garden. 2001. NFB. 94 min. www.nfb.ca. Colour. An intensely personal reflection of Japanese-Canadian history and a testament to one woman's incredible endurance and spirit. Viewable online.

Of Japanese Descent. 1945. NFB. 21 min. www.nfb.ca. The film shows Japanese relocation centers in central British Columbia. This archival film reflects the social and cultural values and beliefs at the time of its production. Available by order.

Sleeping Tigers: The Asahi Baseball Story. 2003. NFB. 51 min. www.nfb.ca. The story of the championship Japanese-Canadian baseball team. Viewable online.

Websites:

www.archives.cbc.ca – Relocation to Redress: The Internment of the Japanese Canadians includes ten television clips and fourteen radio clips.

www.greenwoodmuseum.com – Includes a section on Japanese history and pictures of their exhibits.

www.JapaneseCanadianHistory.net – A list of resources, glossary, and other support materials on the topic of the Japanese Canadian internment.

www.jcnm.ca – The Japanese Canadian National Museum. This site offers online exhibits, resources, and links to many other related materials.

www.najc.ca – The Links page created by the National Association of Japanese Canadians with sections on the histories of Japanese in Canada, the US, and South and Central America.

www.pc.gc.ca/culture/ppa-ahp/itm1-/page03_e.asp – The Nikkei Internment Memorial Centre National Historic Site of Canada in New Denver, BC

toby.library.ubc.ca/subjects/subjpage1.cfm?id=306 – The University of British Columbia's Subject Resources for Japanese Canadian internment

www.lib.washington.edu/subject/Canada/internment/intro.html – The University of Washington holdings relating to the Japanese Canadian internment.

Visual Credits

Ando Hiroshige, artist: p. 10 (1833)

Canadian War Museum: p. 60 (19910109-182), 61 (bottom, 19880069-860), 62 (19750317-062), 64 (top left, 19710135-008; bottom right, 19750317-171), 67 (right, 19910109-177), 76 (left)

Le Canard, Montreal: p. 29 (September 1907)

Charles Kadota, private collection: p. 21 (bottom right)

City of Vancouver Archives: p. 53 (top, Sch P152, by Fred L. Hacking; bottom, CVA 99-4572, by Stuart Thomson), 85 (bottom, CVA 1184-1537, by Jack Lindsay), 121 (bottom, City P5)

C. Tokunaga, private collection: p. 16 (top)

David Suzuki Foundation: p. 140 (bottom right)

D. Tomihiro, private collection: p. 14 (bottom left)

Glenbow Archives: p. 39 (top, NA 387-27)

The Globe, Toronto: p. 28 (October 1907)

Rev. G. Nakayama, private collection: p. 48 (top left)

Greenwood Museum, Wayne Deib Collection: p. 72 (bottom right, 100-2099), 73 (top left, 100-2103), 95 (top, 100-2090), 107 (top right, 100-2101; bottom left, 100-2105), 133 (bottom right, 100-2083), 149 (bottom, 100-2112)

Harry Tanaka, private collection: p. 34 (left)

Helen Tokiwa, private collection: p. 51 (top)

Hou, Charles and Cynthia. *Great Canadian Political Cartoons 1820 to 1914*. Vancouver: Moody's Lookout Press, 1997. p. 18 (top right)

iStockphoto: p. 66, 102 (top), 116, 130 (top)

Japanese Canadian Cultural Centre (JCCC) Collection: cover, p. 11, 20 (inset), 22 (top), 58 (left), 76–77 (bottom), 96 (bottom right), 97 (top), 105 (top), 148 (right), 151 (top, by J. Hemmy)

Japanese Canadian National Museum: cover (96.171.1.001, 94/69.4.29, 94/69.3.018, 94/69.4.16), p. 6 (94/98.2.2), 23 (bottom, kashiten001; top left, 1994-70-6), 25 (top left, 9473007), 32 (94/88.3.001), 35 (bottom left), 46 (top right, 95/102.1.1), 47 (bottom, 96/180.001), 72 (centre), 73 (bottom, 96.171.1.001), 79 (top left), 84 (94/69.4.29), 87 (top, 94/69.3.20), 88 (centre, 94/69.3.018), 89 (1994-69-3-13), 90 (centre left, 1994-69-3-6), 90–91 (94/63.9.023), 94 (bottom left, 97/197.1.002), 98 (94/69.4.16), 100 (top, 94/101.1.007), 105 (bottom, 95/103.1.001), 112 (top, 96/182.1.027), 115 (top left, Kaminishi collection; bottom left, 94/71.1.005), 117 (top, 9481013), 119 (top, 94/134.1.007), 122 (2001-4-4-5-5001, Roy Ito Collection), 123 (top left, 2001-4-7003, Roy Ito Collection; centre left, 2010-53-4, Kenjiro (Okada) Ballard Collection; centre right, 2001-4-4-5-9005, Roy Ito Collection; bottom, 2001-4-4-5-81002, Roy Ito Collection), 126 (bottom, 94/76.003), 131 (1994-93-1-1), 132, 137, 139 (194-83-8), 140 (top), 141 (bottom left, 2002-10-7-d), 144–46

J. K. Shimizu, private collection: p. 21 (centre right)

Kane Inouye, private collection: p. 24 (left)

Ken Kutsukake, private collection: p. 15 (centre right)

Kikuo Kimura, private collection: p. 117 (bottom)

Kogawa House: p. 141 (top)

Langham Cultural Society: p. 79 (top right, 995.002.0311; centre left, 995.002.0233; bottom left, 995.002.0196; bottom right, 995.002.0217)

Larry Scherban, Camera One Photography: p. 67 (left), 150 (top)

Library and Archives Canada: p. 70 (top, PA-114820; bottom, C-049744), 71 (top, PA-114812)

Masako Fukawa, private collection: cover, p. 5 (Mary Ohara, second from top), 15 (bottom left), 21 (top left), 24 (right; centre), 27 (all), 30, 34–35 (top), 43 (bottom), 45 (bottom), 48 (bottom), 59 (bottom right, four images), 67 (top), 93 (bottom), 94 (top), 95 (bottom), 101 (bottom left), 102 (bottom), 106 (top), 114, 115 (top right), 128, 133 (top), 134 (top, by T. Nakatsuka; bottom), 135

The Moon, Toronto: p. 33 (top, April 1903)

Nanaimo Daily Free Press: p. 121 (top right, 1988)

National Association of Japanese Canadians: p. 147 (top, 1128126-04; bottom right, 1128126-01), 151 (bottom, 1128126-06)

New Canadian: p. 120 (right)

Pictorial Encyclopedia of Japanese Culture: The Soul and Heritage of Japan. Gakken, 1987. p. 8–9 (all), 57 (top), 126 (top)

Roger Shimomura, artist: p. 143

Roy Kawamoto, private collection: p. 13 (bottom right)

Sachi Ota, Toronto, private collection: p. 20 (bottom), p. 34 (centre right)

Sara Rainford, Rainfoto Photography: cover, p. 54, 55 (top; bottom), 56, 57 (bottom), 73 (centre right), 83 (all), 97 (bottom), 100 (bottom), 103 (all), 104 (bottom), 107 (top left), 108, 109 (all), 120 (left), 128–29, 136, 142, 148 (left), 149 (top), 150 (bottom)

Sunahara, Ann Gomer. *The Politics of Racism*. Toronto: James Lorimer & Company, 1981. p. 80 (right), 81 (top; centre left; bottom right), 112 (bottom left), 127

Takata, Toyo. *Nikkei Legacy: The Story of Japanese Canadians from Settlement to Today*. Toronto: NC Press Ltd., 1983. p. 16 (bottom), 17 (bottom), 50 (top), 59 (centre left), 74, 75 (right), 87 (bottom left), 99, 106 (bottom), 111 (bottom), 119 (bottom), 130 (bottom)

Takeo Nakano, private collection: p. 113 (bottom)

Tatsumi Iwasa, private collection: p. 21 (top centre)

Terrie Nakamura, private collection: p. 75 (left)

T. Matsuno, private collection: p. 118 (top)

Tom Freeman, artist: p. 68–69

Tom Kawaba, private collection: p. 49

Tosh Kawai, private collection: p. 25 (bottom)

Toyo Takata, private collection: p. 17 (top)

University of British Columbia Archives: p. 51 (bottom), 52 (all, 1916 UBC Annual, courtesy of the AMS Archives), 92

Vancouver Public Library, Special Collections: cover (VPL 3071, VPL 1381), p. 12 (VPL 3019), 13 (top, VPL 3009), 18 (bottom, VPL 7548, by Philip Timms), 19 (top left, top right, VPL 5460, by Philip Timms; centre left, VPL 999; centre right, VPL 71770, by Ben W. Leeson; bottom, VPL 7883, by Leonard Frank), 22 (bottom, VPL 3071), 26 (top, VPL 593; bottom, VPL 21773), 31 (VPL 39046, by N. H. Hawkins), 33 (bottom left, by Philip Timms), 36 (VPL 1869, by William Notman), 37 (top, VPL 2067, by F. Dundas Todd; centre, VPL 2067; bottom, VPL 2110), 38 (left, VPL 86694; bottom right, VPL 86725), 39 (bottom, VPL 13291), 40 (VPL 86024), 41 (top, VPL 2142; bottom, VPL 8433), 42 (VPL 1393), 43 (top, VPL 1397; centre, VPL 2426), 44 (top, VPL 2116; centre right, VPL 2113; bottom, VPL 2173), 45 (top, VPL 86023), 46 (bottom, VPL 11804), 47 (top, VPL 11806), 50 (bottom, VPL 11794), 58 (right, VPL 86007), 59 (top, VPL 86032), 61 (top, VPL 80839), 63 (top, VPL 25766; bottom, VPL 44965), 65 (VPL 8516), 77 (top, VPL 66380), 85 (top left, VPL 1394), 86 (VPL 1346), 88 (inset, VPL 14916), 90 (top, VPL 14927), 93 (top, VPL 1364), 110 (VPL 1381)

Vancouver Sun: p. 80 (bottom left, 1 June 1943)

Victoria Daily Times: p. 71 (bottom, 17 February 1942)

Wikipedia.org: p. 125 (left)

Y. Uyeda, private collection: p. 113 (top left)

Index